THROUGH MY EYES:

A QUARTERBACK'S JOURNEY

THROUGH MY EYES:
A QUARTERBACK'S JOURNEY

BY TIM TEBOW
with Nathan Whitaker

ZONDERVAN®

ZONDERVAN.com/
AUTHORTRACKER
follow your favorite authors

ZONDERVAN

Through My Eyes: A Quarterback's Journey
Copyright © 2011 by Timothy R. Tebow

This title is also available as a Zondervan ebook.
Visit www.zondervan.com/ebooks.

Requests for information should be addressed to:
Zondervan, *Grand Rapids, Michigan* 49530

Library of Congress Cataloging-in-Publication Data is available

ISBN 978-0-310-72345-5

All photos courtesy of the author with the exception of the following (page numbers corre-spond to photo insert):

Page 5 (top and bottom images), Page 6 (all images), Page 8 (all images), Page 9 (all images), Page 10 (top and bottom right images), Page 11 (all images), Page 12 (all images), Page 13 (top image): Courtesy of XOS Digital, Photos by UF Communications, Jim Burgess, Tim Darby, Jay Metz, and Jason Parkhurst
Page 5 (middle image): "Jump Pass" © 2006 by Daniel Stewart
Page 10 (bottom left image): Photo by John Biever/Sports Illustrated/Getty Images
Page 13 (bottom image): AP Photo/Dave Martin
Page 14 (bottom image): AP Photo/Ed Andrieski
Page 15 (top image): AP Photo/Kevin Terrell
Page 15 (bottom image): AP Photo/Marcio Jose Sanchez
Page 16 (top left image): AP Photo/Jack Dempsey
Page 16 (top right image): AP Photo/Jack Dempsey

Typography by Rick Farley
Printed in the United States of America

---

11 12 13 14 15 16 17 18 /DCI/ 20 19 18 17 16 15 14 13 12 11 10 9 8 7 6 5 4 3 2 1

*To all those who have been told that
they couldn't achieve their dreams...*

CONTENTS

1

HEADACHE

And we know that God causes all things to work together for good to those who love God, to those who are called according to His purpose.
—Romans 8:28 (NASB)

MY HEAD was killing me.

It had been a full day already, but as if that weren't enough, now my head was splitting in two. It was horrible timing. I was in New York City for the presentation of the Heisman Trophy, and I'd spent most of the day exploring New York with my family and friends. But it had taken its toll. My head was killing me—a migraine had set in. I guess the travel and schedule had brought it on. I had been traveling nonstop, it seemed, since the conclusion of the regular season a week earlier. I had been blessed enough to win several awards already, including the ones that I was the most proud of, several first-team Academic All-American teams.

The ceremony took place in Times Square, at the Nokia Theatre, as it was then called. There were 2,100 in attendance on December 10, 2008. About twenty of them were pretty nervous for me. Those twenty—my parents, siblings and spouses, close friends, Coach Urban Meyer, and Coach Mickey Marotti from the University of Florida—had been on hand to support me throughout the entire season, as always, in good times and bad.

Statistically, there had been more good than bad that season. I'd thrown for over 2,500 yards with 28 touchdowns and 2 interceptions. I'd also rushed for 564 yards and had 12 touchdowns. But more importantly, as a team, we'd seen far more good than bad as well. We were 12-1 and had only had one close game in the last two months.

Colt McCoy and Sam Bradford were seated beside me on the front row. They had also been nominated for the Heisman, and of course, they had also had great seasons.

We hadn't played either team, yet. We would be facing Oklahoma and Sam Bradford in the BCS National Championship Game a month after the ceremony.

Finally, the moment arrived. As the ceremony unfolded, my head was hurting more and more, and I was feeling nauseated.

The announcement came from the podium, in a moment that none of us would ever forget.

"The Downtown Athletic Club presents the 2008 Heisman Trophy to . . . Sam Bradford, University of Oklahoma."

My phone began vibrating and wouldn't stop for hours—texts and voicemails from teammates and coaches, all saying that we would take it to Oklahoma in the championship game. I wasn't paying attention to the phone, though, as Sam accepted the award—the pounding in my head had continued to intensify.

Finally, at a break, I headed out to the bathroom to run cold water over my face. On the way, I passed Coach Meyer and Coach Marotti. I could feel the intensity of their disappointment and anger over my loss as I approached. They were obviously biased in my favor and were two of my biggest supporters.

I caught their eyes and mouthed two words.

"Game on."

THE EARLY YEARS

Let another praise you, and not your own mouth; a stranger, and not your own lips. —Proverbs 27:2 (NASB)

MY DAD HAS PREACHED a lot in America, but one of his favorite places to preach is a country in Asia called the Philippines. Before I was born, my family was living in Mindanao, in the Philippines, and my dad was doing mission work there. Anyone who talks to others about a personal relationship with Jesus Christ is doing mission work.

One day when my dad was out preaching in the jungle, he prayed, "Father, if You want another preacher in this world, You give him to me. You give me Timmy, and I will raise him to be a preacher."

Dad returned home and told my family about his prayer. He invited them to join him in praying for me by name, and they all prayed for me. The name *Timothy* means "honoring God."

A few months later, my mom realized that she was pregnant. From the start, it was a difficult pregnancy. A number of times they were certain they had lost me. Mom and Dad went to the best doctor in their area of Mindanao and listened to her lay out their options—in her opinion—for how to save my mom's life. The doctor was brutally honest about her opinion of my mom's chances. She said that the pregnancy was going to be hard and dangerous.

When my parents walked out of her office, they were in shock and felt a bit numb. They knew that Mom would have to be very brave and trust God. Her strongest recollection of those moments, which must have been overwhelming for her, was an unexpected and indescribable peace. God's peace, she later told me, is what helped her through the next eight months of her pregnancy.

And while they waited for me to be born, my mom and brothers and sisters would sing Bible verses together. Mom thought that putting verses to tunes helped us to learn and retain them. Later, they taught these verses to me:

Wait for the Lord, be strong and let your heart take courage. Wait for the Lord, wait for the Lord. I wait for the Lord, my soul does wait. And in His Word do I hope.
—Psalm 27:14, 130:5

Miraculously, later on in the pregnancy, a surprise blessing occurred. Mom, who had been very sick, began to feel better, even well enough to fly, along with my siblings, Christy, Katie, Robby, and Peter, to Manila. There, at the Makati Medical Center, she met with an American-trained doctor. She had not seen a doctor for many months.

My family's waiting was over on August 14, 1987, when I was delivered by the doctor my parents trusted. The doctor spoke first to my dad. "Mr. Tebow, your child is a miracle baby. I can't explain how it happened, but despite all odds, he beat them."

My mom, dad, and family were so grateful for my safe arrival and thanked the Lord for His protection of both my mom and me. But the drama was not over yet—for either of us.

That first week, I lost weight instead of gaining it and had to remain in the hospital. My parents asked our friends and family in America to pray that I would grow big and strong. I guess their prayers were answered!

Mom also struggled physically and needed ongoing care, but slowly, she got better.

We are all so grateful Mom survived the pregnancy and childbirth. My parents knew that Mom might not survive, but they trusted God with her pregnancy. Trusting God is how they started their marriage and how they have continued to this day. My dad always tells us that faith is like a muscle. You trust God for the small things and when He comes through, your muscle grows. It grows whether He comes through in ways that you hoped for or not—you learn that He's always there through good or bad. This enables you to trust God for the bigger things, in fact, for all things.

My memories of my life—at least those I myself can remember—begin in Jacksonville, Florida. We returned from the Philippines when I was three.

It was great growing up with two older sisters and two older brothers always around to play with. Actually, all of us were very competitive, including my parents and all my siblings. It didn't matter if it was Monopoly or chess inside with my sisters or baseball or basketball outside with my brothers—or if I was only four and the rest of them were far older. The rules applied equally to all. There was no "letting someone win" because he was younger, or to cheer her up or encourage her to keep playing. The first time I won any of those games or contests, I earned it.

It was something I remembered.

Most of my first clear memories seem to revolve around sports and all the crazy stuff I did trying to be just like Robby and Peter. I wanted to do everything they did, despite the fact that they were nine and six years old when we returned from the Philippines and I was three. We were in constant motion, always playing whatever game was in season or, if for some reason one of those didn't interest us, just the ones that we made up ourselves.

My dad says that I wasn't much fun to throw with, even at age four. Even then I was a bit too intense and threw pretty hard. A lot of my competitiveness was probably just how I was wired, but part of it was because I looked up to my brothers and wanted to be just like them. I wanted to be as strong as my brothers, so when I was a bit older, I used surgical tubing that was attached to the top of the door. My dad wouldn't let me use any weights. He didn't feel they were safe for me at that age. He thought the rubber tubing would produce results that were just as good. While my brothers and I were sitting or standing around talking or doing whatever we were doing—and it was always something—I wasted no time and would stand in front of the door and pull against the tubing, working each shoulder. For thirty minutes or so. Looking back, I'm not sure why I didn't tire of it, but I didn't and simply kept pulling on the tubing, working each shoulder. Over and over.

When it came time to play T-ball at age five, I had already played a lot of actual player pitch with my brothers. The idea of hitting off of a tee didn't interest me. So instead of my using a tee for my at bats, my coach at the Normandy Athletic Association would toss the ball to me underhand, while my brothers took great pride—maybe even more than I did—in watching me hit ball after ball over the fence during the course of the baseball season. Peter claims I hit thirty-six home runs that year. Then again, he was eight at the time and maybe not the best and most unbiased source of information for keeping the records. I know, though, that I finished second in the league in home runs to a kid who was two years older. I made a commitment to myself right then and there that that would be my last year of finishing second.

I do know that I didn't play Little League baseball just for the fun of playing. I can't help it—but that's true. When I hear parents tell their kids today, "It doesn't matter if you win or lose, as long as you have fun," I'm puzzled. That's just not how I'm wired. Bottom line, losing simply isn't any fun. Oh sure, in thinking back on plays and moments, I knew I was loving every minute of playing the game. But if there's a score, then there's a purpose to the game beyond having fun. Of course, there is value in playing the game itself and how well you play it, and always playing to the best of your ability, but at some point, the actual competition has to be a piece of the analysis as well. After all, there'd be no point to the rules or to keeping score if it were simply and only about having fun.

I had two brothers who beat me at everything, at every turn, as badly as they could. So when I played anything with them, I wanted to win. When our coach would say, "I just wanted to make sure you're having fun," I didn't understand. And when my teammates seemed more interested in ice cream or snow cones after the game, especially if it was a game we lost, I was baffled and upset. I couldn't understand why they bothered to play. Just go get dessert without bothering to be on the team, I figured. What's the point?

That outlook may have had an impact on my ability as a teammate back then. In T-ball, I was friends with the other players, and I remember very few of them then who could catch or throw. Early in the games, I would tolerate this, but as it got later and more critical to the outcome, I found myself wanting the ball in my hands.

Once, in the last inning of a close game, the ball was hit to me at shortstop. I fielded it and ran down the runner, who was breaking from third to score, for the final out. After the game, the coach asked me why I didn't throw it to the catcher. The question puzzled me because I thought the answer would have been obvious to him.

"Because he can't catch."

"Well, he's the catcher. You're supposed to throw it to him for him to try and catch it to get the runner out. That's how you do it."

I was sure—no, I was positive—that wasn't how you do it. I wasn't interested in someone's "trying to catch" the ball with the game on the line. I also wasn't interested in someone's trying to remember if he was supposed to tag the base or the runner. If he didn't know what to do, I would do it myself. I would let him try to catch early on, but I wanted to win. When the game was on the line, I would do whatever I had to—within the rules—to win the game.

My parents decided that, with three boys around the house who were as competitive as we were, we had to institute a new rule. I was still young, and they were already concerned about the bragging that we were doing among ourselves. Here was the rule: We were forbidden from talking about our own accomplishments, unless asked first by someone else. If someone specifically asked us how the game went or how we played, we could answer, but we couldn't volunteer the information. They based this new rule on Proverbs 27:2:

Let another praise you, and not your own mouth; a stranger, and not your own lips.

It was a great lesson for us to learn to live our lives with a humble spirit, a lesson we needed to learn and continue to work on. Our parents certainly have always lived their lives with humility.

We did, though, have family friends who knew the rule, and before long, they'd help us out by asking us on a Sunday morning at church, "Any of you boys had any games lately? Anything happen?" And so we would fill them in.

But at the same time, we began to realize that it was nicer to not hear ourselves brag, and so over time, we all just began talking about ourselves less and less.

Plus, we were given a dollar if someone complimented us on our character to Mom or Dad. We quickly became focused on those matters—such as character and humility—rather than on trying to impress someone with our exploits on or off the field.

A year and a half after moving back from the Philippines, my family moved onto a farm. Life on the farm, like anything, had its pros and cons.

The good news? There was plenty of room for batting practice without losing a ball in a neighbor's yard or worrying about a nearby window, and to play whatever other games we wanted to play.

The bad news? My dad made it perfectly clear that

ours was a working family farm, and he and Mom were thrilled to have three healthy boys available every day for all the manual labor life on a farm required.

Actually, even that was good news, as I look back on it. Shortly after we moved, I became "farmer strong," simply from lifting hay bales or chopping wood or chasing down cows.

Dad used to hold batting practice in one corner of the yard, and we dented the fence more than once from pitches that he threw to us or we threw to each other while working on our pitching technique. We would hit balls—for hours on end—toward the tree line on the other side of the pasture. Even with all the extra farm chores we had to do, living on the farm was tremendous. On one occasion, we had a visit from a former White Sox pitcher, Joel Davis. He wasn't going to be able to care for his dog any longer, so he dropped him at our house. The dog, named White Sox because of his white feet, became a family fixture. So did the stories of the balls that Joel hit that day into the tree line across the pasture.

Dad finally wised up before he threw so much that he tore up his shoulder. So he bought some fishnet to make a batting cage. With a number of four-by-four posts, we built what turned out to be a pretty sturdy and functional structure, and then we put a pitching machine in it. From that point forward, we were set. We could pitch to each other to our hearts' content, without fear of losing baseballs to the surrounding woods. All with no further wear and tear on Dad's shoulder.

Somewhere in there, in all the time spent with the stretchy surgical bands or the competitive streak in T-ball or the endless hours of batting practice, I realized that I never wanted to "fit in." As I look back now, it was clear that very early on the seeds of that concept began taking root and sprouting within me in everything I did. As I got older and heard kids talk about wanting to "fit in," or wanting to be "normal," I never quite understood why they felt that way. What's the point of being "normal"? That sounds average to me, and I never felt like I was created to be average.

So if everybody was doing the same thing, the normal and usual thing, I looked for a different way. Members of the crowd don't want to stick out, so they act like everyone else. If we're all special *in the same way*, then nobody really is special. Being like everyone else ignores the fact that we were each created with gifts and abilities like no one else's—and that we can use those unique gifts and abilities to do something special.

You and I were created by God to be so much more than normal. My parents always told us that was true of each of my siblings and me.

Following the crowd is not a winning approach to life. In the end, it's a loser's game, because we never become who we were created to be. I figured that out when I was five, but I couldn't have expressed it then. I just knew that I wanted to be different in those areas that excited me. I wanted to be me—and then I began to understand that I wanted to be who God created me to be.

The most important thing that ever happened to me took place when I was six. At the time, I knew I was ready to invite Jesus into my heart, to accept what He had done for me to allow me to go to heaven.

I tried talking about the decision with my dad first. We talked about Bible verses every day as a family, and I'd heard him preach somewhere around a million times by then. Every time I tried to bring it up with Dad, he would question me on my understanding of the gospel message to make sure I was serious about this big decision. His questions frustrated me!

During that time, I went to bed several nights in a row thinking, *What if I'm in a car accident or something happens tomorrow? I want to go to heaven when I die.*

The year before, I had come close to drowning in the ocean. Some friends of ours took Peter and me to the beach. I was not far from the shore when I was suddenly caught up in a strong current that pulled me into deep water. Eight-year-old Peter ran into the water to save me, but he was immediately caught in the dangerous current as well. He managed to reach me and hold me up long enough for us both to be rescued by the lifeguard. It was a close call.

So one morning several months later, I went straight to Mom after breakfast and exclaimed, "I want to ask Jesus to come into my heart. I am ready to be saved."

Mom and I went over to the couch, and I prayed for Jesus to come into my heart. Since then, I know that I am headed to heaven and have tried to live in a way that pleases Jesus.

We all laugh about it now, but Dad will tell you that he is very glad I went to Mom that morning. That afternoon, we all went to Epcot to celebrate.

3

PREPARING A FOUNDATION

*"For I know the plans I have for you," says the Lord.
"They are plans for good and not for disaster, to give
you a future and a hope." —Jeremiah 29:11 (NLT)*

EVERY YEAR, whatever sport was in season, we played it—
my brothers and I. Since there were only three of us,
we set up certain rotations in order to maintain fair-
ness while still being competitive.

For example, every time it would rain, we'd head
out to play football in the yard. There's something fun
about football and mud. One of us would play quarterback, while the other two would face off against
each other. One would be the receiver and the other
would be the defensive back assigned to cover him.
The receiver would have "four hard," meaning four
downs to score a touchdown. After those four downs,

we'd rotate positions so that each of us would play the three positions at least one time through. If we played longer, we made sure we played all three positions an equal number of times to fairly determine the winner. You'd get a point for scoring whether you were play-ing as the receiver or quarterback, while the defensive back would get a point for stopping you from scoring. In those early days, when we were still fairly small and our bones pretty resilient, we would also play tackle. It may just have been that my brothers only wanted to play tackle until I got bigger.

We didn't have a set score that we played to. Instead, we played until we got called to school, to work or eat, until someone got hurt, until we got into a fight with one another, or it got so dark that we finally could not see well enough to play.

We played basketball in the rain as well, with puddles to navigate through and around as we tried to dribble. And forget hanging on to the ball when shooting. You simply tried to keep your hand as close as possible to the ball—as it began slipping out of your control from being so wet—and long enough to give one last guided push toward the basket with the hopes that somehow it would find its way there. We didn't play in those conditions to make shooting difficult, but I'm convinced those years of informal "wet ball drills" probably helped my skills in both football and basketball.

We weren't always outside, although my mom probably wished we were. We had a version of the old "Oklahoma" drill that every football coach has run at practice at one time or another. We'd play in one of our rooms—usually the room of whoever hadn't been in trouble lately. Two of us would stand at opposite sides of the room, one of us with a football. The third one would watch for Mom, since she had a strict no playing ball in the house rule. He'd also do a bit of refereeing or breaking up a fight, if necessary, while waiting his turn.

On a signal, we'd begin to run at each other, with the idea being that the defender would have to tackle the ball carrier before he reached the other side of the room. Our rooms weren't all that big, so there was quite a lot of wrestling each other down to the floor before the guy with the ball reached the other side of the room.

Someone was always getting hurt when we played—regardless of the game. And it was usually Peter. Once we were playing a three-way game of catch in the yard.

We were each a pretty good distance apart, forming the three points of a rough triangle. Instead of following the pattern that we had followed all that day, where Robby was throwing to me, Robby decided to switch things up. Thinking that Peter was looking, Robby crowhopped and wound up to put his full weight into the throw. Of course, Peter wasn't looking, fully expecting that Robby would be throwing to me, since that had been the pattern that day. With a bloody nose and a bruised face, we took him inside to Mom for some patching up.

Another time, we were playing baseball but decided to use a basketball instead of a baseball just to see what would happen. Nothing good, as it turned out, at least as far as Peter was concerned. I was pitching, and the bat ricocheted with Peter—swinging as hard as he could to see how far he could hit the basketball—right into his face.

More blood. More bruises. Back to see Mom.

Our favorite Peter injury, however, was less about sports and more about one of his moments of pretending he was a superhero. Funny that a kid who is so smart could have done something so crazy. I was about eight when he climbed a rope that had been attached to the ceiling in the barn. He decided to swing from one end of the barn all the way to the other. All went well until his shin discovered, at a high rate of speed, the posthole digger that hadn't been put away and was sitting sideways in the barn, causing his shin to split wide open. Blood was everywhere.

Enter Mom, once again, on the scene.

Living on a farm, there was always a certain amount of excitement around the house, and if it wasn't one of us getting injured, it was the realities of farm life that kept things interesting. On one occasion, my dad decided, this being a working farm and all, to have a controlled burn to get the weeds out of the pasture. Controlled burns were normal but occasional occurrences, and completely necessary in settings such as ours. Apparently "controlled" is in the eye of the fire starter, especially when you don't call the forestry department to forewarn them.

The first indication we had that things were no longer under control was when Dad ran into the house frantically to get our help. As it turned out, the pasture was ablaze, and the fire was moving rapidly toward the woods. If it had reached the woods, it would have been devastating not only to us but to the families around us as well. All of us—Mom, my sisters, my brothers—struck out to help Dad contain the fire.

The fire hadn't yet reached the woods, but we all noticed that it had jumped into our neighbor's pasture. The good thing was that our neighbor would no longer have a weed problem. Hopefully, he would still have a house.

For the next few hours, we used shovels to beat on the edges of the fire. All of us did, although Christy got out of working early. She had a piano audition that day but was worried about leaving us. We all insisted she go, however, and she focused well enough to earn a college scholarship. The rest of us followed in her footsteps, earning scholarships to college, and it's pretty funny that it started that day, during the fire. Even Otis, our dog, was pawing at the flames. Finally, through our collective efforts and what had to be God's grace, we won out.

From that point on, Dad has always called the forestry department for a burn permit ahead of time for a number of good reasons, one of which, no doubt, is that he doesn't have a bunch of kids on hand to help put out any more "controlled" burns. Afterward, Dad took us all inside and used a teachable moment to have a brief Bible study on James 3:1-12. With the smell of the fire still on our clothes, Dad got us glasses of water, sat us down, and picked up his Bible. "Just like a small spark can cause a big fire," Dad said, "the smallest part of the body, the tongue, can cause great damage when we do not control it. A wrongly chosen word can hurt a reputation, alienate a friend, or break a heart." Then he had us each name a word that could hurt someone. A memorable lesson.

In general, all these activities—"controlled burns" and sports—served to toughen us up, usually because no matter what, we wouldn't stop working or playing. Looking back, my injuries were numerous but much less serious than either Robby's or Peter's. I was never as much of a daredevil. But whether we twisted an ankle or cut a chin (my brothers, my dad, and I all have chin scars), the competition and winning was what mattered, so we played through anything. Anything not to quit.

And just as the farm made us tough, it also helped make us smart. As we were growing up, the farm was the backdrop for much of the learning we did—starting when we were toddlers and continuing until we were packing our bags for college. From the moment I was born, homeschooling was our way of life.

Homeschooling seemed like such an obvious choice for our family, but back when my parents first did it, it was far from common. My parents made the decision to homeschool their children long before I came into this world. It happened at some point after my older sister Christy was born, but before she'd started school.

Dad knew he wanted us to homeschool. That way, he and Mom could focus on the curriculum and character lessons that they thought were most important. So they began to pray specifically about it. Dad looked for guidance from God. He wanted to know what decision God wanted him to make on this subject. Mom prayed that God would take the idea out of Dad's mind if it really wasn't the right decision for them as a family.

Ultimately, they both felt led to teach us at home, which at first proved to be really hard for Mom. But Mom was determined to do it right and in the best way possible for us. Her persistence turned out to be a wonderful blessing for all of us, not just because of the quality education we received but also because of the flexibility that it afforded us.

During the sports seasons, they could shift the bulk of the workload to earlier parts of the day so that we didn't have a conflict with any afternoon or evening practices, games, or other activities.

Mom set the curriculum, and she could tailor her teaching to the needs of each of us. She used games or whatever was necessary to reach us and get the lessons across. In our house, school could be happening at any moment, even at meals, so we always had to be prepared. She put different place mats at our places around the table—United States presidents, the periodic-elements table, state and world capitals—and we would be challenged to learn everything on our place mat before the others could. Everything with us always had to be a race or a competition. Mom knew that and used it to enhance our learning process.

My dad had long known that he was dyslexic, but it still took a while before my parents recognized that Robby, too, had dyslexia. By the time I came along, it didn't take them long to spot it in me as well.

Simply put, my brain processes things differently than most people. It's the same for my dad and Robby. All three of us are kinesthetic (or tactile) learners, meaning that we learn best by doing. I don't ordinarily retain as much simply from reading about something. Therefore, I learned to use other ways to supplement my reading to make sure I learned all that I should.

Mom helped me realize that dyslexia wasn't a disability, just a difference. My learning skills and information-processing abilities mean that I learn much more quickly from "walk-throughs," which football coaches love to have anyway. The players literally walk through the plays they will want to execute during the game, and walk through them at a slower speed than actual live-game or practice situations.

Dealing with our dyslexia with wisdom, Mom not only affirmed that we were wonderful creations of God, with our God-given intelligence and abilities, but she gave us the confidence to learn. When subjects came more quickly to me, we could breeze through them, but if they were more of a struggle, we would slow down to focus on them. It was the same with each of my siblings—we were each able to discover alternate and better ways to learn, ways that were unique to us as students.

My mom would read articles to us from the newspaper, or have us read them ourselves as we got older, and then we would identify and discuss the character issues in them. We could always find something to talk about in most every article. As we ate breakfast together as a family, we would read through the Bible. Both of my parents required us to memorize a large number of Bible verses. To help us, Mom would put the verses to music in songs that she had made up.

Don't get me wrong. It was still school—with really small classes: one teacher, one student. My mom gave us grades for every class. She was tough with the amount of work she gave us, but at the end of the day, she was a pretty easy grader, because she was always trying to encourage us. She did insist that we always take year-end tests, however, because she wanted an outside assessment of how we were doing. Also, she and my dad began to suspect I might have a chance at a college scholarship, so they wanted to make sure we all were exposed to testing.

People say that you miss out on things by being homeschooled. But really, I was able to do most everything I needed and wanted to do along the way, and that really helped me develop a sense of accomplishment.

A few weeks before I turned eight, I started playing Pop Warner football near where we lived on the west side of Jacksonville.

The first week of football didn't go all that well. I got

sick every day at practice with headaches, dizziness, and nausea.

At the end of that first week, my parents sat me down. It was clear to them that if these symptoms didn't stop soon, I would have to give up football. It was only a game, and they were not going to medicate me to play a game. Still, I didn't want to give up football, but I'd learned that the Bible says we are all supposed to honor our mothers and fathers. For my siblings and me, it was easy to see that our parents deserved to be honored—whether we always showed it or not. But it wasn't until later—when I wasn't with them all the time—that I began to realize all the reasons that they deserved not only our respect and praise, but to be honored and loved. They cared for us, protected us, and nurtured us so that we could grow into the people God wants us to be. They did whatever it took to make sure following God's wisdom and direction was the path we took.

Well, my mom prayed with me that evening. She and I knelt beside my bunk bed and prayed that if it was God's plan, He might take away whatever it was and heal me so I could play football. And for whatever reason, after that night, I've never had another issue with my head while playing football.

The Lakeshore Athletic Association football program was a great place to grow up and compete. Not only did it give me my first experience at playing quarterback—the only position I've ever wanted to play—it also produced a lot of talent that flowed into the high schools all over the Jacksonville area and beyond.

As much as I loved playing football, I loved playing other sports, too. When I was eleven, I was invited to play on a traveling baseball team, the Tidal Wave. Because they wanted us to try different sports and activities, my parents had always discouraged us from playing only one sport for the entire year; however, they did allow me to play on this traveling team. I played three or four seasons with them, and during that span we won hundreds of games, playing all over Florida and around the country. During the summers, we'd play maybe ten or eleven games a week—with two each Friday, Saturday, and Sunday. I remember many Sundays when we'd leave church and I would change into my uniform in the car as we drove to a game.

My dad never coached us formally in a team setting because of international trips and his irregular schedule. What he did was spend lots of time with us, teaching us not only to hit but also to throw.

Apparently, some people have even commented on that throwing motion.

Dad's fault.

Dad was focused on our overall well-being. Eventually, I felt that I'd taken working out with surgical tubing attached to doors as far as I wanted or could. And I had done push-ups and sit-ups for hours. I wanted to start on weights. My dad kept reminding me that Herschel Walker had turned out to be a pretty fair player with only push-ups and sit-ups, but it didn't convince me—I really wanted to start on weights.

"Not until you get your first pimple," he would tell me. People in the athletic world had convinced my dad that there was no point in training with weights until my body was mature enough and could build muscle through weight training. I had no reason to doubt him, but that didn't stop me from asking. Over and over.

Finally, he gave in. He says it was because my body was ready, while my recollection is that it was just a bit earlier than that. Either way, I finally got a weight set that we kept in the barn. I think Mom felt that if we kept it in the barn, I couldn't damage the furniture or anything else in the house. That was all I had asked for as a Christmas present, and it was a gift that allowed me to change and improve my training regimen. I kept push-ups and sit-ups in my routine, doing 400 of each every day. Dad was still cautious about letting me use any weight heavier than one that I could do at least fifteen repetitions with. He was trying to protect my bones and tendons as they developed and did not want me to hinder my growth.

At some point, still in Little League, I believed and imagined that everyone around me was also trying to improve. In retrospect, I'm not really sure how much most kids were training at that age, but at the time, I was convinced everyone was working hard to get better.

And that's when I adopted one of my mantras—in this case, it was a saying I repeated for getting stronger and better and for all my workouts:

Hard work beats talent when talent doesn't work hard.

Because I assumed that everyone was trying to get better, I began looking for ways that I could get an edge, an advantage that would serve me in competition. I would end up doing things above and beyond whatever was expected to get an edge. I also began working out at odd times of the day and night, thinking,

I'll bet there are no other kids in Jacksonville working out right now. Whether that was actually true didn't really matter—what mattered to me was that I *thought* it was true. It was just another thing that motivated me to work longer and harder.

I'm sure that God made me in such a way that I was willing to work hard, but there was also a lot of encouragement from my parents. They always told me that God had a special plan for me and for each of my sisters and brothers. It was great to know that my parents prayed for me and believed that God had a plan for me.

A FAIR FAREWELL

Whatever you do, do your work heartily, as for the Lord rather than for men. —Colossians 3:23 (NASB)

EVENTUALLY, IT CAME TIME for me to start playing for a school. Since my siblings and I were all homeschooled, we needed a place to participate in sports, and Trinity Christian Academy had been a good home for us for years. We were undefeated during my eighth-grade year, and I was called up to the varsity team at the end of that season. (The varsity season lasts longer.) I didn't play at all that year on the varsity, however, but was biding my time for ninth grade.

Heading into that first year of high school football, we went on a church-planned weekend called the Burly Man Retreat. My family still talks about that weekend.

It probably illustrates as well as anything just how competitive I am.

But there also can be a downside to that competitiveness.

At the end of the night on Saturday, they had scheduled an arm-curl competition. As I remember, it was a fifteen-pound curl bar with two ten-pound weights on each end, weighing in at fifty-five pounds. I kept sliding back in the line as guys were taking their turns, because I was hoping to be the last one to go, in order to know the number to beat.

The number of repetitions that guys were doing kept climbing with each new guy. Thirty-five, forty, fifty. I think it was around fifty-five repetitions by the time it reached the guy who was next to last . . . me. Unfortunately, I wasn't able to slide all the way to the end of the line, so I was going to have to put up a number that the guy behind me—the last guy in the competition—couldn't beat. Better yet, I figured that I'd put up a number that he wouldn't *want* to beat. That way, I'd beat him before he even got started.

And so I began curling the bar as fast as I could. Thankfully, form didn't matter. We just had to raise the bar to our chests however we could. Arching my back, jumping . . . whatever it took. Forty, fifty, sixty, and now I was the leader. I kept going, straight through one hundred, which seemed like a lot, but I wasn't sure. He was really big—the guy behind me, that is.

At 175, my arms were really hurting, but by 225 reps, the pain was pretty much gone and numbness had set in. *May as well keep going,* I remember thinking. I couldn't feel anything anyway and still seemed to have the stamina and energy to go on.

I put down the bar after 315 curls.

I won.

If "winning" had included being able to straighten my arms out afterward, I would've been disqualified. I had to pack that night to leave camp the next day. Both arms were bent stiff at right angles, and when we arrived at church the next morning, I still couldn't straighten them. My biceps were still almost fully contracted from what I had subjected them to in that contest. By the third day, I could finally use my arms again.

I went into my freshman year with a lot of confidence. But then all that changed.

As the season got under way, the coach insisted on

moving me from quarterback to linebacker, despite the success I'd had at quarterback in eighth grade. Now to be clear, this was not the first time I'd had to face this concept. I get it. I always did. I understood where they were coming from. I was a big, strong, athletic kid, and I had an advantage over many of the other kids my age because of it. Coaches would, therefore, always project me to play somewhere else besides quarterback. They all seemed to have a particular body type and lack of athleticism in mind that they associated with that of a quarterback.

Just because I understood this, however, didn't mean I liked it. I always wanted the ball in my hands. I still do. Even in Pee Wee football, they didn't always let me play quarterback. One year, the coach's son played quarterback and I played running back. Another coach thought I was just too athletic to play quarterback. My family was disappointed, too, but they supported the coaches' decisions. They also taught me to have a good attitude and encouraged me to make the best of the situation. I hung with it to be a team player, but I was chomping at the bit to play quarterback. Football was my favorite sport, but what made it fun for me was playing quarterback. Finally, I got to play quarterback again in my fourth year of Pop Warner, and we made it to the championship.

So here we were again. Position by body stereotype. For that ninth-grade year, though, I stuck with it so I could play with my brother during his final season. It was Peter's time to shine. But it wasn't much fun for me.

As I was struggling with the move to defense, I was continuing to work out and get stronger. By that time, too, Robby was in his junior year of football in college, and he started sending me his Carson-Newman College workout books and regimen that the team used. Of course, I always felt that I had to do more repetitions than each exercise called for. I often added to the suggested workouts with additional running or extra exercises or more sets of those recommended exercises. Taken just as it was from Robby's college, it was a solid workout schedule. For me, it was a great starting point.

I didn't realize or ever give much thought to the fact that the body needs a rest period to effectively increase muscle, so for those first few years I made sure I worked out every day. My dad tried to tell me to alternate upper-body and lower-body exercises to give my body a rest, but I'm not sure I always heard him. After all, if four workouts a week were good and the number usually recommended, then seven a week would be much better, right? Eventually, I learned a better approach that would help me to get even stronger and more physically fit.

In addition to the training, I'd also been drinking protein shakes along with my workouts, something that had begun when I was in eighth grade, thanks to home-schooling. The reason I had homeschool to thank was that for months I'd been trying desperately to convince my parents to allow me to use the protein shakes, and for months they'd been resisting. That is until my mom suggested that I do a homeschool project to prove to them that the protein mixtures were safe and necessary. My parents were worried about me taking anything that wasn't simply from a natural food supply or some kind of recognized vitamin. My goal was to use science to persuade my parents that protein shakes were beneficial.

For weeks, I did a lot of research in books, magazines, on the Internet, and at the nearby GNC store, putting together a long and detailed presentation. After all, my athletic preparation was riding on it. In addition, I figured, why not go ahead and try to win the local middle school science fair while I was at it? I tested how much energy I used in a particular workout and how much protein it would take to generate that energy. I even calculated how much protein I could take in through diet alone, and I was able to show that additional sources were necessary in order to get enough protein.

When I was done with my project, I presented it to my parents. It worked. It really was a killer presentation, showing them that the protein shakes from GNC and similar places were completely safe. I had the science to prove it. From that point forward, I was able to use protein along with my working out.

And yes, I won first place in the science fair.

The protein shakes, though, were just the start. I paid a lot of attention to what went into my body, and around this time I also decided to give up soft drinks for a year. My parents had witnessed over and over how committed I was to taking care of and improving my health. So they decided to challenge me, talking with me about their concerns about the detrimental effects of ingesting too many carbonated drinks. They even backed it up with their own research. As an enticement to quit, they offered me one hundred dollars if I went without having any soft drinks for a full year. I did it.

I should have held out for more money, but in the end, it was worth it. To this day, I still don't drink soft drinks.

While watching my diet and working out in the right way helped me train, much of my early strength came from working on the farm. Some days, it was just for an hour before we'd begin schooling. Other days, it might be all day, especially if there was a particular project on the farm that needed our immediate attention. We put up fences, chased and herded cows back to where they should be, planted gardens, felled and cleared trees that were dead, chopped firewood, and did whatever other work that needed doing on the farm.

In the end, though, being farmer strong, being trained, taking care of my body—it all felt like it would be futile if I couldn't play quarterback. Despite the fact that I kept improving and had good practices when I was allowed to play at quarterback, the coaches still used a different starting quarterback. That was how my freshman fall at Trinity went, and as the season came to a close, my future as a Trinity quarterback didn't look very bright. I continued to play hard and did what I was told at linebacker and tight end.

• • •

Between football, homeschooling, and farm chores, I kept pretty busy. I was also involved in activities at church. Starting in second grade, I had special parts in the children's musicals. My first role, however, did not take much acting ability since I was the back end of a camel! In third grade, I was a sailor, and then I went on to be a Supreme Court judge. In fifth grade, I was chosen to play Superman. That was fun, and the costume was pretty cool. But a problem arose because dress rehearsal was at the same time as the semifinals for the city baseball championship.

My mom and I prayed (Dad was in the Philippines), and my team won without me. That meant, however, that the championship game was the same time as my musical. We prayed again. To their credit, my coaches made an appeal to the city, and the final game, which we won, was changed to Monday.

Baseball was probably my best sport and the one that seemed to come most naturally to me. I had played varsity since the seventh grade. And I was still enjoying being on the Trinity baseball team, as well as the basketball team. We even played some golf. It was expensive to go to a golf course, so we figured out a way to play at home. Dad let us take the weed whacker out into the pasture and create our own putting greens. Then we used the posthole digger to make the cups. We were able to create four holes on our own farm this way. One of them was even a water hole over the pond.

As much as I enjoyed playing sports for Trinity, though, my parents and I were still troubled with the quarterback situation at the school. And so we came to the conclusion that the time had come for us to look for other schools where I could play football. It was a disappointment to us all, but somehow we all knew it was the right thing to do.

My sophomore year, I played for a different school, Nease High School in Ponte Vedra Beach. Coach Craig Howard began his first year as head coach, and I started at quarterback. This was the first year in ten years that the school had a break-even season. We scored a lot of points against bigger and faster opponents, and that helped to build our confidence for the next year.

I resolved to work as hard as ever and did my best, through my words and my example, to challenge my teammates to reach for something much more for themselves and the team.

PHILIPPINES, FOOTBALL, FAITH, AND OTIS

Therefore, go and make disciples of all the nations, baptizing them in the name of the Father and the Son and the Holy Spirit. Teach these new disciples to obey all the commands I have given you. And be sure of this: I am with you always, even to the end of the age.
—Matthew 28:19-20 (NLT)

WHEN YOU'RE YOUNGER, every birthday feels like a milestone, and the summer of my fifteenth was no different. For many reasons, I was excited to turn fifteen, but perhaps the most important was that turning fifteen meant I was old enough to go on my first mission trip to the Philippines the following summer. For years, my dad had been leading a mission trip to the Philippines in July, and finally I'd be able to go, too.

That's how we were raised, with a joy in getting to tell people about Jesus. For as long as I can remember, this was instilled in me: to have fun, love Jesus and others, and tell them about Him.

I hadn't been back to the Philippines myself since we'd moved to Florida when I was three. But I had grown up with my dad making frequent trips back to the Philippines. And Richard Fowler, who was a huge part of my life when I was a little kid, also understood how important the Philippines was to our family and how important it is to help those who are less fortunate.

Uncle Dick, as we called him, was important to our whole family. I met him when my family got back from the Philippines when I was three. We spent nearly every Saturday morning at his house—probably because he owned a TV and we didn't. We ended up over there on weekdays, too. He let us drink the small bottles of Coke in his refrigerator and eat the Popsicles from his freezer. Our parents have told us on numerous occasions that Uncle Dick loved our visits. I have no doubt that he did—I mean, after all, who wouldn't love five brothers and sisters descending upon your house and food supply on a regular basis? I loved going over there, and he was truly a member of our family. In fact, he spent every Thanksgiving and Christmas with us. And I'm named after him—Timothy Richard Tebow.

My family's relationship with Uncle Dick began before I was born. In 1982, my dad began a church out of our house. That first Sunday, Uncle Dick was the only person in the living room whose name wasn't "Tebow." Uncle Dick became a member of the new church, and our friendship with him was off and running.

When Uncle Dick died, he left a lot of money to support an orphanage that my dad founded, and we renamed it "Uncle Dick's Home." Uncle Dick left a great legacy behind him when he did that. So when it was my turn to go on a mission trip to the Philippines, I was really excited for a lot of different reasons. I knew that going to the Philippines would be a challenge, but what I did not expect was that it would change my life.

America and the Philippines have had a long friendship. With the permission of school principals and other school leaders, we missionaries connect our purpose to the moral and spiritual values program already in place in the schools. We emphasize the love of God and a personal relationship with Jesus Christ, and staying away from drugs.

When possible, we have an assembly with the whole

student body, such as at their morning flag ceremony. At an assembly, we have a short ten to twelve-minute message of the love of God. If we are unable to have an assembly, we share the same message classroom by classroom, which is much more speaking, but the small size of the group makes what we're saying more personal. We almost always have a minute to shake hands and high-five students, which is a special time. (Perhaps this is where my tradition of high-fiving Florida fans after each game began.)

My dad gets us up around 4:30 a.m. each school day to get ready and eat breakfast. Then we get on the road, often traveling very far to get to the first school. We usually have two or three Americans on a team with two Filipino staff. The staff drives, does most of the talking to the principals, and then translates the message to make sure everyone understands all parts of the message.

We work hard all day until school is out. It is fun but exhausting. In a typical day, a team will speak in six to ten schools. Sometimes fewer and sometimes more. When I am speaking, I usually open with comments about being born in the Philippines. That creates a great connection with students.

Then I talk about the gospel. The word "gospel" means "good news." So I ask, "Do you like good news?" Of course, they respond, "Yes." "The good news is that God loves you! He loves you so much that He sent His Son Jesus to die for you. He made you special and wants to have a personal relationship with you and give you eternal life. But our biggest problem is that we have sinned. Because God is a Holy God, He cannot be around sin. Sin makes a wall between God and us. Because Jesus had no sin, He could die for our sins on the cross. Because Jesus died on the cross for your sins and rose from the dead, He has the power to forgive your sins, make you His child, and give you a home in heaven. That is the best news you could ever hear. You can't earn the free gift of eternal life, you can't pay for the free gift of eternal life, you can only receive it as a free gift, by putting your trust in Jesus Christ alone."

And then I always end with an invitation to pray with me if they want to trust Jesus. I pray something like this: "Dear Jesus, I know I am a sinner and need a Savior. Thank you for dying on the cross for me. I open the door of my heart and ask you to come in. Save me now, Jesus. Thank you for saving me. Thank you for coming into my heart. Thank you that God is my Father and I am His child. Thank you that I have a home in heaven, and I will come and live with you some day. In Jesus' name, Amen."

Finally, I ask them several questions. "Did you ask Jesus into your heart?" "Where is Jesus right now?" "Is He ever going to leave you?" "He promised to never leave you, to never forsake you, to be with you forever. If you have Jesus and you died today, where would you be?" "If God is your Father and God is my Father, what does that make us?"

Personally it is so exciting to have the privilege to share God's love with other people. One special day, I spoke in nine schools to 29,000 people. The first school that day was over 11,000 students. Needless to say, it was a wonderful day in the schools.

Many nights, I got back to the hotel we were staying in with a terrible sore throat. As I fell asleep, I thought there was no way I'd be able to speak the next morning. But every time, I woke up refreshed and ready to go.

The mission trip was also great preparation for the speaking I would end up doing as I got older. Speaking without notes, learning to make my remarks shorter or longer depending on the amount of time I had, adjusting my remarks based on the size of the group—my work in the Philippines provided great training for it all. I now actually prefer speaking without notes, because it gives me a chance to engage my audience with my eyes and my gestures. Without notes, I'm also assured that my comments will be real, authentic, and come from the heart.

Full days. Packed classrooms and auditoriums. Being worn out at the end of the day. That's what our trips back to the Philippines were like. But we loved it, and I came back from my first mission trip to the Philippines renewed to fulfill my purpose of living for the Lord, whether here or there and in whatever place, setting, or game I found myself in.

Life was good back in the States, too, when we returned from the Philippines. For the most part, life was quiet for us other than my schooling, working on the farm, and playing sports.

In order to register at my new school, my mom and I had started living in a family apartment away from our main house. One of the hardest parts about this was that it meant I was apart from Otis, our beloved dog. We got Otis when I was five years old. He was loyal and protective, traits you'd hope to find in a dog. If you came by, you would be greeted by blond-haired Otis, a mixture of half Lab and half golden retriever. He would wander our property, looking for threats to the family, including snakes. When he found one, he would eliminate the threat and then leave the dead snake for us—probably so we could see that he was keeping us safe. He must have done this a hundred times.

Otis met every visitor who came onto our property, whether invited or not, and usually before anyone else in the family had the chance. Our guests or any delivery truck or our large-animal vet—anyone and everyone—were all escorted—chased, really—as they came up the driveway toward the house. He was always keeping an eye out for us and *on* all others.

For my birthday weekend in August that year, I went with my brother Robby and good friend Kevin to Disney World. When we returned home after the weekend, something seemed different as we drove onto the property.

My mom met us as we pulled up in front of the house. Noticeably upset, she said, "I haven't seen Otis all weekend."

That's what it was. That's what seemed out of place. Otis always greeted everyone, excited to see friends and strangers. That's what was different. He wasn't there when we pulled up. And now Mom was telling us he seemed to have been gone all weekend. It wasn't completely out of the ordinary for him to take off for several hours, but never several days.

Getting more upset by the minute, I took off on foot, running around the farm, then decided that the car would be faster. So I got in and started driving around the property, calling as loud as I could, over and over again, for Otis. We covered the entire property as well as some property off the farm, even though Otis had never left the farm before. I went back and forth, over and over, hoping at any moment Otis would come bounding and barking from behind the corner of somewhere—maybe even with a harmless snake hanging from his mouth. I smiled, thinking for a moment about what a welcome sight that would be.

I drove slowly down the driveway again, looking toward the underbrush on either side. There it was— that golden head popping up in the brush. I slammed on the brakes, jumped out of the car, yelled for the others, and ran toward him, calling out to him as I ran.

He put his head back down. In the past, he would have always come running to greet me. I reached him, afraid that maybe he'd been bitten by a snake. He looked fine, and I slowly and gently lifted his head. I still didn't see anything wrong, until he opened his mouth.

It was bleeding badly, and he was missing teeth. I looked down at his legs and realized that instead of being tucked under him as they should be and usually were, they were awkwardly splayed around him. Otis had been hurt badly, but I couldn't figure out by what.

I gently but quickly scooped him up, put him on the seat of the car, and raced back to the house to tell the others, so we could all head to the vet. And all the way to the vet, I was getting more and more upset and more and more frustrated with the state Otis was in. It appeared to me that he'd been hit by a car or kicked by a cow.

The vet told me that Otis's back, legs, hips, and jaw were all severely damaged. Surgery would have been extensive and expensive, and there was absolutely no guarantee that at his age he would survive the surgery or actually get better after it.

So we brought Otis home to die and laid him carefully on his bed.

Only we forgot to tell Otis that was the plan. We forgot to tell him that these were his last days.

So, every day, I carefully lifted Otis and carried him to the pool. He had grown up swimming in our pool and our pond, but this was a bit different, and he seemed to know it. He didn't fight getting in the pool, but it didn't excite him, either, as it had in the past. I put him on my lap and gently lowered him into the water up to his shoulders. We just rested in the pool in that position together for a while, and then I would carefully take him back into the house. Neither one of us was prepared to give up.

When I'd been doing that for a couple of weeks, I began gently moving his back legs and watching his reaction. We took it slowly and increased his movement over time to help his muscles regain some tone and strength. He didn't seem to want to move them on his own, so I would move them for him—and he let me. Over time, I started moving my hand out from under his back legs, which would force him to begin to paddle a bit to feel like he was staying afloat. I never took my hand off his chest and never made him paddle much. Just long enough so he could take a few strokes with his legs and regain some confidence and strength in them.

It was hard to look at him, though, without feeling how painful it all must have been for him and how he still must have hurt. Every time I looked at him, I could sense and feel the pain he was in.

Thankfully, Otis continued to get better. Over the next few months, with the regular pool workouts and lots of milk shakes—he loved vanilla—he regained the ability to walk again. He never ran again, but he settled back into being himself, even though as a bit more frail version of the original Otis. But he was our Otis—the one we always knew and loved.

• • •

A couple of weeks later, football season began. It was my second football season at Nease, and we continued to make great strides to improve during my junior year.

This year, expectations were higher for all of us—including me. The previous year, my playing had gotten a few colleges to quietly notice me, and I was hoping to give them reason to make some real noise about my abilities.

But more important than wanting interest from college coaches, I felt a lot of responsibility for helping to make our team better and for pushing all of us to fulfill our potential. It was Coach Howard's second year as head coach at Nease High School. He'd had a full year to encourage us, set the bar higher for us, and persuade us that his way would lead to success. He'd also had some time to build his values and lessons into us, including one that he taught and reminded us about often: "Our job as coaches is to love you guys; it's your job to love each other."

And as time passed, they did just that with all the players, and we did with one another. It all began to make a difference—both on and off the field. In the next round of the playoffs, we faced our nemesis, Saint Augustine. We had faced them in the regular season, knowing that we had a good chance to beat them, but lost by a slim margin. This time, we were so jacked up and believed we were ready for this game. It was going to be the perfect setting for finally breaking through to beat them—we had lost twelve straight games to them.

It was back and forth early. Then our turnovers contributed to their taking a big lead. We were so far behind by halftime that it seemed like we had no shot at getting back into the game. To our credit, though, nobody in our locker room lost heart, and we continued to scrap and battle, slowly chipping away at their lead.

Finally, we had driven close to their end zone and trailed 35-28 with just seconds left on the clock.

I kept the ball on a power-keeper play and lunged halfway across the goal line in the middle of a pile of bodies. The referees never made a call one way or another, continuing to unpile players. While they were unstacking players, they never stopped the clock. When they finally got to the bottom of the pile, they should have found me with my entire upper body and the ball across the goal line, but somehow they didn't see it that way. Instead, they ruled that the ball never got across the goal line.

No touchdown.

No time left.

Game over—11-2 for the season, with both losses to Saint Augustine.

Saint Augustine raced off the field jumping up and down, cheering and hollering in celebration, while we stood there, in stunned silence. Our season was over.

Through the off-season and the summer, we kept growing together as a team, and by my senior year, in 2005, we were an incredibly tight-knit group—brothers-in-arms ready to go out together to face whatever was before us. We had all gone to camp together that summer to work on our football, a commitment that some had avoided in the past. We began meeting every Wednesday night and talking about important things, something pretty rare among high school students, even rarer especially since we were guys. We were truly trying to live out our coach's mantra:

CHARACTER
STRENGTH
HONOR

Coach posted those words on the locker room wall. Every day they were right there, in our faces. After that 11–2 record of improvement capping my junior year, we now had even higher expectations for my senior year.

At the same time, there was a lot of attention on me and whether I would perform at the level everyone expected. In the lead-up to the season, I'd learned that there was going to be a documentary about me, which was scheduled for broadcast on ESPN. It was very flattering that they would want to do that, and even though it was very well done, I was pretty embarrassed by it. And the title was the worst part of the embarrassment: *The Chosen One*.

They interviewed coaches, teammates, and other key people from my life. And while I didn't really want the extra attention, it turned out to be really fun. And because of all of the attention, it also led to other players getting scholarships.

But I'd have at least changed the title.

We breezed through our regular season, with scores like 70-21, 49-13, and 53-0.

But then Saint Augustine was a different story. They scored twenty points early in our game, and in a steady rain, our rally fell short, 20-14. We had battled back and forced a punt late in the game to give us a chance, but we were penalized for roughing the punter and never got the ball back. We simply dug too big of a hole for ourselves early in the game. Mike Shula, the man who was head football coach at Alabama at that time, watched it all from the sidelines, as some of the Florida college coaches sat in the stands.

Same outcome as always when it came to Saint Augustine. I joked that I didn't want to have something like that in common with Peyton Manning. He had a great college career, but his Tennessee Volunteers could never beat the Florida Gators in their four tries. I was wrong, as I lost four times to Saint Augustine.

Hopefully, I can find other ways to mirror Peyton's career.

It wasn't funny at the time, however. Losses crush me. I work so hard off the field and am so physically exhausted after games that I've been known to cry at times after losses, and occasionally even at wins. I just get so exhausted after games—not to mention that I'm pretty sensitive—that all the emotions just flood out of me. It just happens. It's the way God made me.

Of course, plenty of people have seen the other side of me as well, the way that I get so intense and fired up during a game. That's a challenge for me—becoming so intense and yet still staying in control enough to show good sportsmanship. That's something my parents have worked on with me for years.

Thank goodness, Saint Augustine was not in our district that year. We won every game in our district and headed for the play-offs. In the next-to-last regular-season game, I suffered a high ankle sprain, which hampered my running ability. I wore a hard cast over my ankle and focused on passing in the first playoff game against Leesburg. I threw four touchdown passes in the first five plays and then sat out the rest of the game.

The next playoff team, New Smyrna Beach High School, did not expect me to run either. We were losing late in the fourth quarter. With two yards to go on a fourth down, Coach Howard let me run, and we scored. I ran one more time, and behind some great blocking, we scored then too. We survived to move on to the next round of the playoffs.

My leg was much better when we played our next playoff game against Eastside High School in Gainesville, and I rushed for 62 yards. Since Eastside now had to defend the running threat, our offense was freed up, allowing me to throw for over 400 yards.

The following week, we played Pensacola Pace, who was highly favored to win. It was an intense game at our stadium with a record crowd. In the crowd were many of the Alabama coaches, while Coach Meyer paced the sidelines, making comments to my two brothers. Near the end of the game, we used a play that Coach Howard had gotten from the University of Florida—"Bullets." I threw a 99-yard touchdown using that play.

After winning that game, we got to play Armwood High School in the 4A State Championship in the Miami Dolphin's stadium. Armwood had won the state championship the previous two years and were hoping to make it three straight. We were considered to be the biggest underdog in all of the state championship games.

Our offense was solid, though, and as a result, I had a good game, passing for over 200 yards and four touchdowns, and rushing for 193 yards more and two touchdowns. Those six touchdowns set a Florida championship game record. It was a phenomenal feeling as the coaches, staff, team, fans, and school celebrated the achievement that our hard work had brought to us. Because of Coach Howard and his staff, as well as the commitment that all of us as players had to one another and to the success of our program, we won the state championship.

Along the way, I'd also managed to shape a high school career I could be proud of. By the time I was done, I had been named to the First Team All-State team twice and was named 2005 Mr. Florida Football. With the support of my teammates, I set career marks in Florida for total offense, passing yards, touchdowns, and completed passes. I also now held the single-season records in Florida for total offense, passing yards, touchdown passes, and total touchdowns. I had worked hard, and my coaches and teammates had worked hard, but I had also been richly blessed by God and by so many around me, who made me better as a person and student-athlete.

The day after we'd won it all, my mind had already moved elsewhere. It was now time for me to turn my attention to deciding what college I would choose. Earlier in the fall, I'd committed myself to making a decision by that next week, and I had no idea what I should do.

And Otis heard about it all.

WHERE TO GO, WHERE TO GO?

Trust in the Lord with all your heart; do not depend on your own understanding. Seek His will in all you do, and He will show you which path to take.
—Proverbs 3:5-6 (NLT)

ONE DAY DURING my sophomore year, I came home and found the first of many recruiting letters. One was from Ohio State, and the other one was from Louisville. I was so jacked.

They arrived on a Monday, and as I sat with my parents that night watching *Monday Night Football*, I couldn't help myself—I was still so excited about my first-ever recruiting letters. And so when the players introduced themselves at the start of the game—"LaDainian Tomlinson, Texas Christian University"—I tried it out for myself from the security of my couch.

"Tim Tebow, University of Louisville."

"Tim Tebow, Louisville."

"Tim Tebow, THE Ohio State University."

It was a fantastic night, rereading those two letters, watching the game with my parents, and daydreaming about someday playing college football—and who knows what else after that. We were laughing, having fun dreaming about it throughout the game. I still think it's pretty fun to think about introducing myself for a *Monday Night Football* game.

As it turns out, the letters didn't stop with those first two.

Instead, they continued to roll in, creating quite an impressive stack of interest over time. Lots of schools, and lots of conferences. The University of Maryland, the University of North Carolina, North Carolina State, Florida State University, Miami, Michigan State, Notre Dame, Ole Miss, Iowa, Illinois, Ohio State, Oklahoma, Oklahoma State, Colorado, and others. By the time I had graduated, I had over eighty scholarship offers from schools across the country. When I started high school, I was simply hoping for one. It was a very humbling as well as exciting experience.

One school seemed to have had an advantage initially for me—Alabama, because of its fans.

Seriously. The University of Alabama fans. Honest to goodness, a crowd of them used to come to our games at Nease High School in their red-and-white Roll Tide gear. They held up homemade signs for me and encouraged me to head to 'Bama. I'd always liked the idea of a Southern school, not to mention one that was football crazy. It was very influential on this young and impressionable player.

And it needed to be effective, since I grew up in a room decorated in Florida Gator stuff. Orange and blue colors on all sorts of objects and outfits had been decorating the walls, tables, and closets around our home for as long as I could remember. Of course, it was only natural that I would grow up with Gator stuff, since both my parents and my older sister Katie attended the University of Florida. And by my sophomore year of high school, Peter was already in Gainesville and enrolled in school there. Three graduates of the University of Florida and another on his way, all in one family.

Given that background, you'd think that this would be the easiest decision in the world, but in truth I was pretty open-minded about schools since I was such a big college-football fan in general. I'd grown up watching just about every game I could on Saturdays—that is, when Dad didn't make us work around the farm. So I was willing to consider other options besides Florida.

Looking back, I like to think I chose what school to go to based on better reasons than recruiting letters, fan or family apparel, or where everyone else was going.

Throughout the process of visiting colleges and talking to coaches, Coach Meyer from the University of Florida and I became very close. He said he'd first heard of me when he arrived in Gainesville at the University of Florida in December of 2004, as their new head coach. Then, a few weeks later, he attended a coaches' convention in Louisville, Kentucky. He said my coaches from Nease High School were everywhere in their green-and-gold shirts, helping to keep me foremost on Coach Meyer's mind.

That following spring of 2005, my junior year in high school, he'd seen me for the first time in person during a Nease baseball game. We both remember that game, but for different reasons. It was the district championship game against Saint Augustine. I homered in the last inning to win it. (I couldn't beat them in football, but baseball was a different story.) Coach Meyer said that he remembered observing my leadership during the game and on the field. He said he'd never seen a right fielder impact his team the way I did. Whether I really did or not, I'm glad that *he* thought I did.

Simply put, Coach Meyer loves football and loves winning. That was a good place to start for me. No matter what was going on, he was always engaging and enjoyable to speak with, and yet somehow he was able to balance that by being totally focused on championships. He possessed an overwhelming drive and determination to win championships—so strong that I had no doubt he would succeed.

My official visit to Florida was impressive to all my family members who attended: Mom, Dad, Robby, Peter, my sister Katie, and her husband, Gannon Shepherd. Four of the six were Gator grads and Florida beat FSU that day.

On the other hand, Mike Shula, the Alabama coach who had come to see me play in that final Saint Augustine game, was always very clear about how he viewed me and what he wanted me to do. He was also focused on championships at Alabama and returning them to their prior levels of success. More low-key than Coach

Meyer, his faith and that of his staff was appealing. Many of the position coaches, for instance, prayed with their players. I enjoyed that—and in my experience it was unique.

Those coaches, as well as some of the others I've mentioned, stood out for their honesty and integrity. That's why I faced a difficult decision.

I told each of the coaches who were recruiting me that I would decide by the middle of December, shortly after we finished our season. I picked that time for two reasons. First, because of homeschool, I had the flexibility to start college early. Wherever I ended up, I wanted to begin in January so I could participate in spring practice. Second, I wanted to help my college recruit other players if I could and if it would be helpful. By deciding early, I could try to help convince others to attend with me and, in the process, hopefully increase our chances of winning championships in the future.

Unfortunately, the decision to attend early meant I also faced a difficult decision about continuing to play other sports. My dad really wanted me to play baseball my senior year. Baseball had continued to be the sport at which I felt I was most naturally gifted. I was named to the All-State team my junior year, and we went to the state championship. Dad kept pushing baseball and had been making a compelling argument since I was young: If you're good enough to have a professional career in baseball, it's usually longer than a football career. Injuries are less frequent, and the pay is greater.

He was right, and I did love baseball. Turning and connecting on an inside fastball is a great feeling.

But football was my *passion*. More specifically, playing football as a throwing quarterback has always been my passion, and I was not going to let baseball get in the way of my making a timely decision.

Decision Day rolled around, and I still didn't know what I was going to do. Earlier in the day, I had already called Coach Miles at LSU, Coach Carr at Michigan, and Coach Carroll at USC. I told them I appreciated their time and interest but that I wouldn't be coming to their school that next year. It was down to the final two, Alabama and Florida. I had been praying about it regularly, as was my family. I had no doubt that the Lord was leading me throughout this whole process, but what was unclear was determining where He was leading.

People often seem to think that when we follow the Lord, our paths will always be clear, the decisions smooth and easy, and we will live a happily-ever-after life. Sometimes that may be true, but sometimes it's not. Bad things still happen to believers, and good things happen to nonbelievers. When it comes to making our decisions, God wants us to live by His Word, the Bible, and trust Him.

But that's part of faith, what the writer of the book of Hebrews describes as a belief in things that we cannot see. Still, it would have helped if He had yelled down from heaven the direction He wanted me to take or had just written the answer with His fingertip in the clouds—I certainly would have been listening and watching.

Postponing my decision wasn't going to help. I wasn't going to grow further apart from either Coach Meyer or Coach Shula in the next two months. Most likely the opposite would occur. If anything, the decision would grow even harder.

Therefore, on Tuesday, December 13, 2005, just three days after we had beaten Armwood High School to win the State 4A title, I stood behind the stage with my parents and family. No one could help me decide— my family understood my dilemma. I am sensitive to the way others feel and didn't want to tell either of these two coaches *no*. More importantly, I actually wanted to play for both of them.

We had just filmed the presentation of the Florida Dairy Farmers High School Player of the Year in the school auditorium and took a break before news crews were to film my college decision. The crowd and cameras were ready. We were not.

Thirty minutes until showtime. Still no idea. I was overcome with emotion and trying, unsuccessfully, not to cry behind the stage. It had been a long, arduous, and, at times, emotional journey. I wanted to make the right decision.

Twenty minutes. I owed them answers.

I gulped and picked one.

"I'm going to Florida," I told my dad. "I'm going to call Mike Shula first and let him know."

I called Coach Shula. As I told him I was going to Florida, my tears turned into sobs. I doubt he could make out anything I was trying to say, but he was getting the point. He cut me off.

"Tim," he began, "I love you as a person and a player. When I told you that you were going to have a great career and life of meaning, I meant that. I wanted it to be here, but it's still true. I still love you, and you're still going to do great things, even if it's not at Alabama."

I have no idea what I said to him after that, but we hung up and I turned to my family.

"That's the coach I want to play for—Coach Shula's so great. Maybe I should call him back and change my answer." First, though, we decided, I should speak to Coach Meyer and see how that left me feeling.

"Coach, it's Timmy." He laughed nervously, as if he didn't know who was calling. He told me he'd been driving around much of the day to stay busy while waiting for my call. In fact, he had been trying to stay busy all day, but every turn brought him back to my decision, he said. He had gone for a jog that morning and passed several runners who called out, "Hope you get Tebow!" Then, at the office, Jeremy Foley, the athletic director at Florida, stuck his head in.

"Any word from Tim Tebow?"

Of course, there was no news. He'd then headed out into the stands at Florida Field, where he sat on the forty-fifth row. Forty-five was his lucky number, and since he couldn't think of anything else to do . . .

Finally, as he was stuck in traffic, I called.

"Coach," I continued, "I've been thinking about it,

and . . . Coach? Are you there? Coach?" He wasn't. Dead silence on the other end of the line. I later learned that his phone had died after he'd been driving around and using it all day and that he didn't have his car charger with him.

Now I had no idea what to do. I was thinking, *Do I stick with Florida since that had been my final and maybe knee-jerk reaction, or do I switch to Alabama based on the always-classy Coach Shula? But if I do that, shouldn't I tell Coach Meyer first that I'm not going to come to Florida?* I couldn't get through on his phone and didn't know why.

I took the podium and quieted myself and focused. Earlier in the day, I had typed my prepared statement with a long list of thank-yous. I concluded my statement with "Next year, I will be playing football at the University of _____." I had left it blank, trying to decide.

Ninety miles away from that podium over in Gainesville, Shelley Meyer called her husband in from outside. She had the television on. Coach Meyer had driven home and was playing catch with their son, Nate, nervously passing the few remaining minutes until the announcement.

ESPN had put the microphone on me before we went on the air, and I could see the cameraman's look of amazement as I turned to my family members, trying to decide at the last minute where to go. Coach Meyer's passion flashed into my mind.

"I will be playing college football next year at the University of Florida." There, it was done, and the peace that I had been waiting for throughout this whole process was still nowhere to be found. But, at least, the decision had been made.

Unfortunately, it wouldn't turn out to be the last time I cried over a Florida–Alabama outcome.

7

RUNNING DOWN A DREAM

Therefore, since we are surrounded by such a huge crowd of witnesses to the life of faith, let us strip off every weight that slows us down, especially the sin that so easily trips us up. And let us run with endurance the race God has set before us. We do this by keeping our eyes on Jesus, the champion who initiates and perfects our faith. Because of the joy awaiting Him, He endured the cross, disregarding its shame. Now He is seated in the place of honor beside God's throne.
—Hebrews 12:1-2 (NLT)

AND SO IT WAS OVER. But then, it continued.

My entire football career has been so blessed, and as you will read, I have had the opportunity to be part of some great teams, great plays, and great games. As I begin to describe the events of my college career, please know I do not mean to sound boastful as I am always aware that every great play, my talents, and abilities are all gifts from God.

Florida's 2005 season had been good by most standards—9-3 overall, tied for second in the SEC Eastern Division—but not by Coach Meyer's standards. It was his first year at UF, and he made it clear that he wanted the incoming freshman class to help the program do better.

I wanted to prepare for the 2006 season in any way I could. In the weeks before I made my commitment to Florida, I'd spoken to Coach Meyer about skipping my spring baseball season at Nease to enroll early at Florida.

Then about two weeks after I committed, Coach Meyer called and suggested that maybe I would want to play baseball with my high school teammates one last time instead of showing up early at Florida.

"What's going on, Coach?" I was confused, because Coach Meyer had been excited about my plan to enroll early. He explained. In the recruiting process, no one had blinked about my homeschooling, but now the admissions office was concerned—not about schoolwork or test scores. Those were fine. They were simply hesitant.

Two weeks after I'd committed, it was still unclear if I was going to start at Florida in January or if I'd have to begin in the fall with the other freshmen. Coach Meyer was also concerned that I might become a professional baseball player if I didn't enroll. The day before I was supposed to go to UF, I still didn't know if I could. Then I got word from Coach Meyer that everything was arranged. It turns out, he talked to the university president directly and personally guaranteed my academic performance.

As of the next day, I was going to Florida.

I arrived at the University of Florida that January. The night before my first class, I caught a ride to Gainesville with Peter in his pickup truck. I carried only a duffel bag's worth of possessions with me.

I slept on Peter's couch in his apartment for a few hours until I had to head over to our first workout in the wee hours of the morning. Football started right away—even before classes. We met that morning in the team meeting room in Florida Field. Then I had to shift gears and head off to my first class.

My first class at Florida was in public speaking. I had an advantage over most of my classmates, because of all the times I'd already spoken in the Philippines.

Two weeks later, I went to the old Florida Gym, affectionately nicknamed Alligator Alley, for the first of our off-season workouts. It was mid-January, very early in the morning, and still dark out. I was totally fired up. By now, that shouldn't surprise anyone.

The gym used to be where the school played basketball. Now it was Coach Mickey Marotti's personal torture chamber. He was the head of the team's strength-and-conditioning training. I'd first met Coach Marotti during the recruiting process. I had also heard the stories of his legendary workouts.

On that first day, I learned to love Coach Marotti's mat drills. Love. We had done a version of mat drills at Nease High School, but these in Alligator Alley were far more intense. To be more accurate, the mat drills were awful.

That first day, after spending forty-five minutes on conditioning and quickness drills, we did some mat drills to finish the hour. The drills pitted one player against another, each reaching the point of complete exhaustion. I was pleased, however. I hadn't lost one drill. So far, so good.

One morning during conditioning drills, I was paired with a defensive tackle in tug-of-war. Every time I'd done tug-of-war in the past, the winner had to pull the other guy over a line. But this tug-of-war lasted until one of us gave up.

We battled against each other and neither gave up. Eventually, my opponent lost his balance and fell down. But he didn't quit. I dragged him hanging off the end of the rope. He still didn't concede. I kept walking and dragging until I reached the wall. Still didn't concede. By that time, he had scrambled back onto his feet. As he did, I saw that I was next to the door to the men's room. I kicked the door open and kept pulling and pulling, backing my way into the room. I did the same thing once I reached a stall door. Kicking it open, I continued to pull on the rope, hand over hand. I pulled him into the bathroom and toward the stall. Finally, when I had pulled him into the stall with me, Coach Mick blew the whistle and brought an end to the drill.

All those drills were great for helping the team mentally as well as physically. Because for the next four years, whenever we took the field, we knew that our opponent hadn't gone through anything similar to what we had. Coach Mick's mindset and my mantra went well together:

Somewhere he is out there, training while I am not. One day, when we meet, he will win.

We were the ones doing the extra work, and we knew it.

GETTING MY FEET WET IN THE SWAMP

Now godliness with contentment is great gain.
—1 Timothy 6:6 (NKJV)

BEFORE I KNEW IT, our opening home game against Southern Mississippi had arrived. I remember how excited I was to walk off the bus to the field through the Gator Walk, surrounded by thousands of energized fans. To run out of the tunnel onto the field for the first time and to be a part of all the excitement was incredible. Putting on the uniform with my new number, 15, and heading out for my first pre-game warm-ups as a Gator was an indescribable experience. As we gathered in the tunnel, seeing the footage of live alligators on the video board and hearing the voiceover, "The Swamp. Only Gators get out alive," the crowd worked itself into a frenzy! It all still seemed like my childhood dream, but it was one that my teammates and I were living.

Finally, the voice of the Gators boomed "Heeeeeeeeere come the Gators!" as we rushed out of the tunnel. Coming out of the tunnel with "Tebow" on my back for the very first time was such a thrill for me and for my whole family. The goose bumps were everywhere. Something you think about your whole life, and then in a surreal rush, it's actually happening. I felt blessed.

Chris Leak was the starting quarterback. He was a senior and knew the system. From the sidelines, I listened to the fans singing "We Are the Boys of Old Florida." Then we were just beginning the fourth quarter when we got a turnover on about their six yard line. So I wasn't surprised when I got the call to go in. I was nervous calling the play, but once the ball was snapped, all the nervousness went away.

The ball was snapped way low and to the left, so I ran and picked it up. I didn't even think—I just reacted to the situation, which was fun. I picked the ball up, ran left, stiff-armed a guy, dove, and laid out toward the end zone, scoring a touchdown. After I scored, my excitement bubbled over as I just kept running around and giving everybody a hug. I was so pumped up.

The next week, we played Central Florida. I went into the game during the second quarter and had some success. I handed off to Kestahn Moore once we got down close to the end zone, and he scored—a good start for me. I did, however, throw an interception, too. Anytime you throw a pick in a game, it stays with you for a while.

After that game, no one was ever again allowed to tackle me in practice. For me, that was a sign that the coaches knew I could play quarterback at the University of Florida.

The coaches now had a different attitude toward my ability to play quarterback. Leading up to the Tennessee game, they put together some plays just for me.

On the first play they called for me, I ran with the ball. I looked into their safety's eyes and thought, *He doesn't want any part of this*. He went for my ankles and made a good tackle, a solid tackle. It was at that moment that I knew I could play in the SEC. He was one of the better safeties in the conference, and he chose to go low for my ankles rather than try to take me on straight up.

In the fourth quarter, we were losing 20-14 and

facing fourth and nearly two yards, Coach Meyer called a time-out. I was standing there in front of him, staring at him. I'm sure he was thinking, *He's only a freshman*, but he didn't hesitate in sending me out there. As I ran onto the field, all I could think was, *Holy cow, this is the loudest place I have ever been in*. The crowd was going crazy.

I just kept thinking, *I have to get this, I have to get this. I'm going to run as fast as I can, downhill*. I thought of Coach Mick and those mat drills. *They're going to take some punishment*.

I clapped my hands, took the snap, and quickly hit the hole, the gap between the midfield players and the front strikers, running as fast as I could. I knew we had gotten the first down. I was so jacked up that I popped off the ground as we unpiled.

When it was all over, we had beaten Tennessee, 21-20, and in my first Southeastern Conference game, I had really helped the team win a big game.

That next weekend, Kentucky visited the Swamp, and we all knew that we couldn't have a letdown after such a big win against Tennessee the week before. On my first three plays, I had long runs of twenty and thirty yards, taking us down to inside Kentucky's ten yard line.

Later in the game, I faked to the right, and then I spun around to the left and threw to Dallas Baker. We scored on it—my first touchdown pass in college—but they called holding on Phil Trautwein. As we came back into the huddle, Phil, who was a sophomore, apologized to me. Of course, he hadn't meant to be penalized. I looked him in the eye and said, "No problem. That was only my first passing touchdown in college *ever*—don't worry about it." That became a joke between us that I still remind him of.

The next week was Alabama, again at home. When I went in, we had a fourth down and goal to go from the one yard line. Someone hit me at the line of scrimmage, but I had such momentum that I carried him into the end zone with me. That was a sweet feeling, to do that at home against Alabama.

Later in the game, I threw the ball down the sideline and completed it deep into their territory. We continued down the field and scored on that drive. I didn't have many plays in that game, but the ones that I did have were pretty big.

The following week, we faced our fourth straight

SEC game, against Louisiana State University. Early in the LSU game, they put me in. And on my first play, I almost scored a touchdown, except a guy tripped me at the last second. Throughout the first half, the momentum and advantage kept swinging back and forth—first to us, then to them, and back again to us.

Then we got to try the now-famous "jump pass." When I ran it in practice, I ran it wrong the first time—when I got the ball, I faked the run by running almost all the way to the line of scrimmage, but then I stopped, jumped, and threw the ball to the receiver who had worked his way into the back of the end zone. It worked, and the coaches decided to keep it in the game plan as a jump pass.

We got the ball with a minute or so to go in the half and drove down the field to inside the ten yard line. Coach put me in and told me, "Either throw a touchdown pass, or throw it out of bounds. *Don't get tackled, and don't come down with the ball.*"

After the snap, my go-to receiver on the play was held coming off the line of scrimmage. He finally broke free, but he was stumbling, so I just lobbed it in the air to the spot close to where I was calculating he'd end up. The receiver Tate Casey reached out as the ball floated toward the ground, and he caught it in his lap for a touchdown.

Coming out of the locker room for the second half, we got the ball early in the third quarter in great field position. I was put in the game. I completed a pass to Louis Murphy, who was able to take two steps and fall into the end zone.

We won the game, 23-10.

There we stood after the first six games—undefeated. All the momentum was still behind us, and the potential out in front of us.

ENDING UP IN THE DESERT

Always be joyful. Never stop praying. Be thankful in all circumstances, for this is God's will for you who belong to Christ Jesus. —1 Thessalonians 5:16-18 (NLT)

AFTER THE LSU GAME, my family and friends went to Outback for dinner. What my parents remember most about that night was that I took the time to talk to a really sweet but shy little boy who approached our table. I always have time for little kids, the kind of time people like Uncle Dick had taken with me. My dad commented on that experience by saying, "You were on the ESPN *GameDay* set after the game. They showed everyone in the country your jump pass, but your time with that little guy was your best play of the day."

I was really looking forward to the game at Auburn University.

My first play of the game, I ran for the touchdown. The game went back and forth between us. I played on only about three snaps. The rest of the time, I was watching from the sidelines and feeling that I could help the team more. What made it worse was that we did not play well. As a result, we ended up losing to a team that we shouldn't have, 27-17. After the game, a reporter asked me how I would handle the loss. I gave him the verse that my parents taught us:

In everything give thanks; for this is God's will for you in Christ Jesus.
—I Thessalonians 5:18

Six wins and one loss.

We had a week off from playing, so the team tried to get refocused. Then we headed to Jacksonville for our sixth SEC game in a row. I was looking forward to that week because it was the Florida-Georgia game. I had grown up going to that game every year, so I was excited to finally play in it.

I was ready. I went into the game on the first drive and had a really good run. I played on and off for the rest of the game, but the worst part of the game for me came in the second half. I fumbled the ball, and it was recovered by Georgia on our own ten yard line. They scored to cut our lead to seven. I was mad at myself. We hung on to win, 21-14, but didn't play very well offensively that day.

Chris Leak still started in our game at Vanderbilt, of course. I did play a little more, and it went well, including a thirty-yard run.

Early on, things were clicking on offense. After a while, though, we stopped moving the ball effectively. They mounted a comeback and scored thirteen unanswered points in the fourth quarter. Chris struggled, throwing three interceptions, which was totally out of character for him. Toward the end of the game, Vanderbilt scored, but we won, 25-19.

The day after the game, Robby called. It was a call I knew could come at any time, but I still wasn't ready for what he told me—it was so hard to hear that our beloved, faithful, and protective Otis had died. The limp had gotten better over time, but he had cancer and was thirteen years old. Because of football, I couldn't go home to help bury him. He was a great dog, and a great friend. Robby buried him down by the lake on the farm. Otis was an incredibly tough loss, and it was even more difficult because I was away from home.

We were in the middle of a tough streak. We were winning, but we weren't playing very well. We were still focused on getting to the SEC Championship Game and winning that, but we weren't certain we could achieve anything more—such as the national championship. There were a number of teams around the country who had lost only one game, and they were all playing pretty well. We were just barely hanging on in games even though we ended up winning—except for Auburn, of course. It just seemed as though it was going to take something special to really fire us up and get the juices flowing again.

When South Carolina visited the Swamp, things didn't change much. Other than a second-quarter touchdown, we just weren't moving the ball the way we'd planned.

Still tied 7-7 early in the fourth quarter, the coaches called a play for me to try and get the first down. I overthrew it by about a foot, so we had to punt, which was very frustrating and typical of the way the game was going.

South Carolina took the lead, 16–10, with eight minutes to go. We blocked the extra point—and with four minutes left, we started what seemed like it could turn out to be our final drive of the game. We faced a fourth and two from our own end of the field. They might have been able to run the clock out if we didn't get the first down to be able to keep the ball and keep the drive alive. We called 97 Q Power. For a brief moment, I saw nothing but daylight on the play, but then a guy crashed into me from the side. Despite that, we gained enough for the first down and kept the ball. We kept moving down the field, and eventually we had the ball at South Carolina's twelve yard line.

We needed a touchdown. Coach Mullen called a run play for me. I jump-stepped over their safety at the five yard line, like a hurdler, dashing in for the score. The extra point was good, and we led 17–16. Then South Carolina moved the ball down to our thirty-one yard line and lined up for a forty-eight-yard field-goal attempt for the win.

By that point, I was praying full-time. We were holding hands on the sidelines, and when Ryan Succop went in to set up to try the kick, I just closed my eyes. I didn't want to watch—I was just praying and praying. To be honest, in that moment, I don't even know exactly what I was praying—I was just praying.

I'm not sure God is into who wins or loses—He probably is more concerned with what you do in the process and what you will do with either result, to glorify Him and change the world by hopefully impacting one life. But since my parents raised me to pray about anything that's on my heart, I pray—even if some of those things seem minor compared to some of the other big stuff that goes on in life.

All of a sudden, I heard the crowd erupt. I opened my eyes to see Tony Joiner running to get the ball, and I realized from where he picked it up that it must have been blocked. I later learned that Jarvis Moss blocked his second kick of the day—preventing a crushing loss and securing a spot for us in the SEC Championship.

The bench unloaded as we all just ran out onto the field. We celebrated for a long time on the field, a lot longer it seemed than ever before.

Our 62-0 win over Western Carolina that next week wasn't the most exciting one for the fans that year, but I got to play the second half and really enjoyed it. Coach Meyer let me make checks at the line and call audibles, calls that change the play on the line. He didn't really restrict me when we were winning. He just let me go ahead and play.

Before the team could focus on the SEC Championship Game, we had to beat Florida State. I grew up really not liking FSU. I had vivid memories of them beating us and ending Florida's undefeated season on Thanksgiving weekend of 1996. But then I remembered how nice it was when Florida returned the favor the next year in Gainesville and we won.

It was close at the start of the game, and as is often the case with this rivalry, the advantage kept switching back and forth from us to them. We got the ball at our one yard line, and they put me in. After the snap, no one stopped the nose guard. He came through and met me about two yards deep in the end zone.

My brain was screaming that I couldn't take a safety. I think the score was tied at the time 7–7. I was thinking, *I will not be the reason Florida ever loses to Florida State.* I hit him with all I had and began driving him forward, thinking, *No, no, I can't take a safety.* Later on, when we reviewed the film, it was pretty neat to watch my obvious determination. I'm driving him so hard that you can see his knees just snap back and he ends up flat on his back. I got the ball to the half yard line. Barely out of the end zone, but out. It wasn't the breathing room the coaches were hoping for, but it was back out of the end zone.

Otherwise, I didn't get a lot of plays in the FSU game. I got a few short-yardage plays and was able to help us out on most of those.

We continued to drive down, and Chris threw to Dallas Baker to win the game 21–14. Our defense played well, and it was just more of the same story of that year. It wasn't always pretty, but we survived and somehow came away with a win.

With FSU behind us, the next and biggest hurdle came against number-eight Arkansas in the SEC Championship Game. Going into the game, we were ranked fourth in the country. Ohio State (number one) had already finished their season, and USC (number two) was a heavy favorite to beat UCLA that same day. A win would earn USC the right to meet Ohio State in the Bowl Championship Series (BCS) National Championship Game in January of 2007.

During warm-ups, we were quite focused. As the game got under way, we jumped on them early in the second quarter. Chris scored on a running play, and our defensive scheme was awesome and executed to perfection. We took a 17-7 lead into halftime. Then Coach Meyer told us the news: UCLA had just beaten USC, 13-9. If we won, we could very well be playing for the national championship.

Arkansas, however, had different plans, and in the second half they came back to take the lead from us. After that, the game was back and forth. Clinging to a three-point lead in the fourth quarter, we drove the ball down to the Arkansas five yard line. At that point, Coach put me in for a play that we had practiced all that week: I faked a handoff, then faked running toward the line of scrimmage. Then I pitched it back to Bubba Caldwell, who had circled back from his wide-out position. Bubba then threw a pass to Tate Casey, who was wide open in the end zone, and that put the game away.

We won the seventh SEC title in Florida history by a score of 38-28.

The next day, we learned that we would play undefeated Ohio State, the number-one team in the country, in the BCS National Championship Game.

As you would expect, my whole family—except for Katie and her husband, Gannon, who were about to have a baby—went to Glendale, Arizona, for the BCS National Championship Game. They had a great time touring and visiting the area, while my time was pretty much taken up with practice and game-related activities.

I wasn't particularly nervous. I was excited, but that energy came from hoping I would play a lot.

Although we felt we were ready, you never know how you will perform after a month without playing a game. Sure enough, the game started with Ohio State's running the opening kickoff back to the end zone. Touchdown, Ohio State.

There we were—down 7-0 before we could even catch our breath after warm-ups. We had been hearing a lot of people talk about how much better Ohio State was. We were sick of hearing that, but the opening kickoff seemed to support that idea.

But only for about eight seconds.

Instead of folding, we took their kickoff and marched the ball right down the field. Then Chris Leak threw a touchdown pass to Dallas Baker to tie the game at seven apiece. That got the momentum on our side. I ran once during that drive and a couple of times on the next possession—after our defense forced Ohio State to punt after three plays. We scored on that drive as well, to take a 14-7 lead. Our defense was shutting them down. We were blitzing everybody, bringing a bunch of guys at a time. I doubt they had ever seen a defense with that much speed. We were shutting them down from every angle.

We added to our lead, and then with a few minutes left to go in the second quarter, and with us already ahead 27-14, we got possession of the ball. Chris then completed a few passes and got down to the one yard line. When the coaches called another one of my plays, I went in. Bubba Caldwell was wide open for the pass I threw—another touchdown, and we led 34-14 at the half.

The second half, I got to play even more. Midway through the fourth quarter, we got near the goal line again. I stood in Coach Meyer's line of sight yelling, "I'll score! I'll score!" He put me in, and I scored, finishing with one touchdown passing and one touchdown running.

Most importantly, we won the second national championship in school history, 41-14. Chris played very well and was named MVP of the BCS National Championship Game. Well deserved. I was happy for him, a senior, ending it on a good note.

We flew back, and those flights are really just the best. I hate flying, but after a game like that, you look forward to those flights. There's something about being together after all the work you put in— celebrating and thinking and talking about all you accomplished together.

Upon returning to Gainesville, we had the Gator celebration in the Swamp at UF. It was remarkable to be able to watch everything and see the thousands of fans gathered and be with them. Growing up, I had a DVD of the 1996 National Championship year, which I watched all the time. I remembered Coach Spurrier, who was the coach then, had everyone chanting, "*We're number one.*" Now that was us.

10

STARTING OVER

Don't worry about anything; instead, pray about every-thing. Tell God what you need, and thank Him for all He has done. Then you will experience God's peace, which exceeds anything we can understand. His peace will guard your hearts and minds as you live in Christ Jesus. —Philippians 4:6-7 (NLT)

OUR OFF-SEASON wasn't all that bright or positive. When we got back to campus in January after the national championship, the team took a few days off. Soon, both classes and training for spring practice began. Right away, it seemed like a lot of guys were being a bit lazy when it came to defending our national championship. We had all worked so hard during that 2006 season and had been recognized nationally for our efforts. More importantly, we now had a stage from which to influence kids and others for good. It was something that I believed we should take seriously and build upon. A lot of my teammates agreed and came ready to go. But too many others seemed to have a different attitude. That attitude seemed to say, "I earned my role last year and am entitled to it. I intend to claim it and enjoy it." And some of the new players on the team liked the fact that they were coming onto a team with history. What they didn't all realize, though, was that this history was earned off the sweat and sacrifice of others—not by them.

In other words, we did not appear to have the sense of commitment that had helped us win the national championship. I may have been particularly sensitive to what I saw as a drop-off in commitment that spring because I was entering the year as the starting quarterback. We weren't nearly as talented in 2007, especially on defense, and needed to work really hard.

We simply didn't have enough guys who were workers, committed to the sacrifice it would take.

I solidified my position as the starting quarterback heading into the summer. I wanted to do everything I could, however, to make sure I was ready to do my best, so Coach Mick worked with me individually a number of times. He'd try to see how close he could come to breaking me. Actually, he probably wanted to see if he *could* break me.

One of the things he loved to do was have me squat with my thighs parallel to the floor and my back against the wall—like I was sitting in an invisible chair. He would then start to stack forty-five-pound plates and sandbags on my thighs and yell, "Don't you move! Hold it! Hold it! I'll tell you when we're done!" I would hold it until my body was shaking and ready to collapse, and he'd then—usually—release me.

Still it wasn't all work.

One night during that off-season, I had just finished my homework when four of my friends pulled up in a car. They told me about a Kenny Chesney concert and invited me to go with them. The problem was, they didn't have tickets; but they were hoping they could use my influence to get all of us in!

I thought it would be a challenge to get in, and I was right. As we stood outside the building, a security guard recognized me. Later, he brought out one of Kenny Chesney's managers, who invited me and one other onto Kenny's bus. My friends started arguing, and we could not figure out who should go with me. Finally, he told us all to come aboard the bus.

We got to chat with Kenny before the show and were able to get into the concert! During the show, he brought me and one of my friends onto the stage, where Kenny asked me to say a few words. Then he asked if we knew the words to one of his songs. I'm not a singer, so more than anything I did the Gator chomp a few times and swayed side to side. By the end, Kenny put on a UF football helmet—even though he's a Tennessee fan. Hey, sooner or later, we all end up as Gator fans, right?

Our first game of the season was against Western Kentucky, and for that entire week I was pumped, since it would be my first game as a starter. That moment of coming to the Swamp as the starting quarterback was something I'd looked forward to all off-season. Actually, I'd looked forward to it my whole life.

Things went pretty well. We played how we needed to against a team that was clearly not as good as we were. As a result, we won my first start. I ended up passing for exactly 300 yards.

I know people said the teams we played outside of our conference were too easy, but our next opponent,

Troy, had a solid team. We knew we needed to start out strong and try to get an early lead by playing well and hard. We did and ended up scoring every time we had the ball in the first half, building a lead of 49-7 by halftime. In the second half, we came out totally unfocused, and they began to chip into our lead. After Troy quickly scored seventeen points to start the half, we finally regained our focus enough to keep them from winning. Final score—59-31.

I had butterflies in my stomach as we prepared to take the field against Tennessee that week. The Swamp was going crazy. It felt like the fans didn't stop cheering and shouting from pre-game until the game was finally finished. Thank goodness! We needed every one of them.

The Volunteers got the ball first, but our defense stopped them on three plays. They punted to us. Brandon James was electrifying as he got the ball and ran the punt back eighty-three yards for a touchdown. The whole stadium was shaking.

It was a lead we would never give up.

Going into the second half, the score was 28-13. We received the opening kickoff and got a great drive going. We marched the ball down the field, deep into

The baby of the family: My mom and my brothers and sisters with me shortly after I was born.

I had football on my mind from a very early age.

With my mom.

When I was growing up, my brothers and I were inseparable. Once we moved to the farm, we'd play just about any sport we could together.

Playing football in the yard with Uncle Dick.

Uncle Dick's love and generosity provided a start for the orphanage in the Philippines that was eventually named after him.

Here I am with my favorite teacher, my mom.

No matter what sport I was playing, I only knew how to play one way: hard.

With our beloved family dog, Otis. Whenever we came home, he was there to greet us.

When I first played football, I played at the Lakeshore Athletic Association in Jacksonville.

With my brothers after a church play.

Life on the farm made our entire family "farmer strong."

When I was fifteen I went with my family on the first of many mission trips to the Philippines. It was my first time back since I was three years old.

With my dad (left) and Coach Howard (right), my high school coach at Nease.

2006, Florida versus Southern Mississippi:
My first touchdown as a Florida Gator.

2006, Florida versus LSU: The first
jump-pass touchdown of my career.
("Jump Pass" © 2006 Daniel Stewart)

Florida Gators, 2006 National Champions.

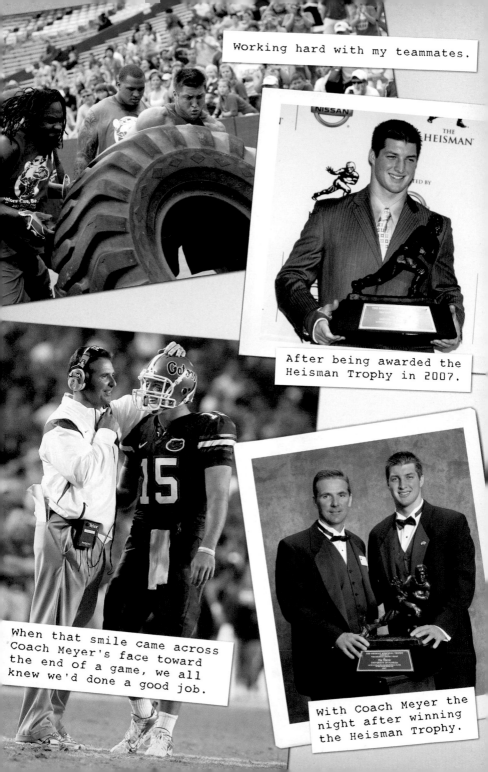

Working hard with my teammates.

After being awarded the Heisman Trophy in 2007.

When that smile came across Coach Meyer's face toward the end of a game, we all knew we'd done a good job.

With Coach Meyer the night after winning the Heisman Trophy.

Hanging out with fellow SEC Heisman Trophy-winner Herschel Walker during the Heisman weekend festivities.

With our dear family friend and one of my favorite people in the world, Uncle Bill.

Throughout college I continued to take mission trips back to the Philippines. Being at Uncle Dick's Orphanage with all of the kids is always an amazing experience.

When I'm in the Philippines, speaking in front of large groups is a terrific way to spread God's message of hope and salvation to as many people as possible.

A promise was made . . .

. . . and now it was time to back it up.

There's nothing like Florida versus Georgia—especially since it's in my hometown.

2008, Florida versus the team out West: This was my favorite game against them. . . .

The more it rained, the more we Gators felt like we were at . . .

. . . the Swamp.

Jump pass to seal the victory in the 2008
National Championship Game versus Oklahoma.

Giving thanks.

The only personal foul of my
career—and it was worth it.

As a team, we had accomplished our goal.

Florida Gators, 2008 National Champions.

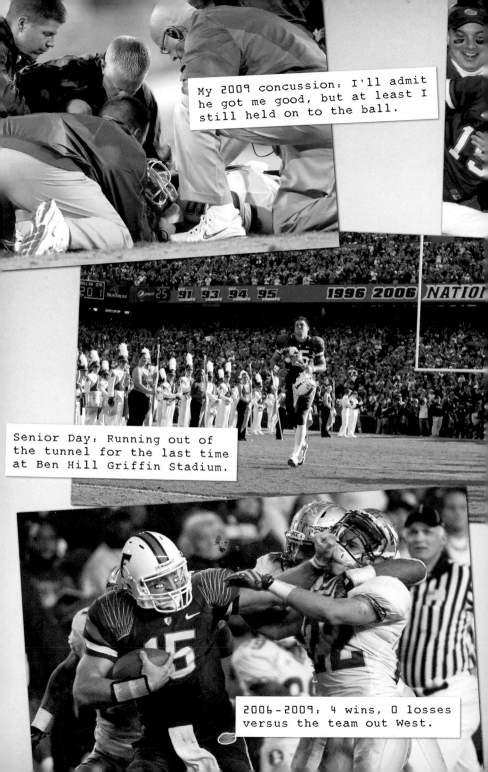

My 2009 concussion: I'll admit he got me good, but at least I still held on to the ball.

Senior Day: Running out of the tunnel for the last time at Ben Hill Griffin Stadium.

2006-2009: 4 wins, 0 losses versus the team out West.

WILL MISS ITS SUPERMAN

My last victory lap at the Swamp.

TEBOW 15

With my parents at my graduation from the University of Florida.

2010 Sugar Bowl: Florida 51, Cincinnati 24. We finished strong. Thank you, Gator Nation.

Draft night in Jacksonville, Florida, with my brothers and friends (from left to right: Peter, Bryan Craun, Robby, Kevin Albers, Angel Gonzalez).

My first day as a Denver Bronco. Excited to still be wearing blue and orange.

October 10, 2010,
Broncos versus Jets:
My first NFL touchdown.

December 19, 2010,
Broncos versus Raiders:
My first NFL start.

December 26, 2010,
Broncos versus Texans:
My first home start . . .

. . . and it was
a great comeback win
for our team.

2010—the Tebows and the
newest addition to our
family, my dog Bronco.

their territory, and hoped to put the game away with a pass down the middle of the field to Riley Cooper. I threw to Coop—and Tennessee intercepted the ball, running ninety-three yards for a touchdown.

It was now 28-20, and they forced us to punt. On the handoff from the Tennessee quarterback, their running back fumbled the ball. One of our linebackers picked it up in full stride and took it all the way back to the goal line. With that touchdown, we were up fifteen, and from that point, we proceeded to bury them with an unexpectedly lopsided 59-20 win.

To win my first SEC start at quarterback made me feel like I definitely had a purpose. Tennessee was a good team—and we demolished them. I ended up with four touchdowns—two in the air and two on the ground. Personally, it felt really good, but what felt better was that we'd done it together. It had been a team effort and a huge win for us.

The good feelings lasted one more week, but we could do better, even in a win. We beat The University of Mississippi, in my first start away from the Swamp, 30-24.

I ended up with some surprisingly big numbers for the game against Ole Miss, throwing for over 250 yards and rushing 27 times for 168 yards. I scored two touchdowns passing and two rushing. As a result, I was named the SEC Offensive Player of the Week for the second time that year.

Now it was time to prepare for our game against Auburn just one week away. Unfortunately, we didn't realize how prepared we needed to be.

Honestly, Auburn didn't seem like a particularly good team in 2007. However, for the second year in a row against Auburn, things didn't go our way—immediately.

Auburn played with more passion as the game began. Every time they got the ball, they were holding it, making first downs and running the clock down. They scored twice in the first half, and it was 14-0 at halftime.

After the half, we really needed a touchdown, but Auburn's defense kept us from scoring, so we had to kick a field goal.

We kept fighting and finally tied it with two touchdowns in the fourth quarter at 17-17. Then Auburn kicked a game-ending field goal to beat us at home, 20-17.

It was so frustrating because we had the ball with an opportunity to win and I couldn't get it done. Right or wrong, I blamed myself for the loss. I'd let everyone down.

I was praying a lot at different times in that game,

too. I know God doesn't necessarily prefer one outcome over another, and He was making it clear. It was
an answer to prayer—just not the answer I wanted.

The next night, Coach Meyer and I had a long talk,
mostly about handling defeat. His words were quite
helpful to me. We read Bible verses together, focusing
on how God won't give us more than we can handle.
We spoke about how God has a plan for our lives and
our lives together as a team. As we talked, we both realized that we didn't feel we'd played our best. I think it
was good for us both that night to think about football
in a spiritual way and to know that God will help us
handle whatever challenges He gives us.

Of course, Coach Meyer and I also talked about the
game some. In the game against Auburn, I felt like I could
have helped before we got into second and third down.

The competitor in me wanted to say, *Just give me
the ball all three plays and let's see what happens.*
Instead, we had a good talk about how we'd handle it
the next time and how we'd handle this loss from this
point. It was a good opportunity for Coach and me to
have that bonding experience and to be able to talk
about those things that matter most.

I felt really blessed again.

COMMUNICATION PROBLEMS

Be kind to one another, tenderhearted, forgiving each other, just as God in Christ also has forgiven you.
—Ephesians 4:32 (NASB)

THAT WEEK was a tough one. There were so many distractions, it's amazing I got anything done. Dealing with the Auburn loss was hard enough, but what was even worse was the game coming up. The following Saturday would be my first trip back to Tiger Stadium in Baton Rouge since my recruiting visit my senior year of high school.

The week of the game, some LSU fan got my phone number and gave it out. I was told that there were announcements around Baton Rouge along the lines of, "This is Tim Tebow's number. Call or text him and give him a hard time." They did. My cell phone vibrated nonstop. Hundreds of calls and text messages were being sent every hour, and the battery was dying every 90 minutes or so. I probably exerted too much energy dealing with communication problems and other crazy fan-related issues.

Coming into the game, LSU was ranked number two in the country, and some say they had one of the best defenses ever in college football. But we opened the game playing like the better team.

We kicked a field goal on our opening drive and wouldn't let them move the ball farther down the field, which forced them to punt. After that, we drove the length of the field again, down to their two yard line. I faked the run, bootlegged out to the left after faking a handoff to the right, and looked for Kestahn Moore in the end zone. He was covered. I kept running all the way to the sideline, looking for someone to come free. Then I stopped, backed up for just a moment, and tucked the ball with my arm. That's when the three guys around Kestahn finally stepped up for just a split second, thinking I was getting ready to run it in. At that moment, Kestahn came open, and I threw it to him. He made an amazing grab around his knees for the touchdown. The kick for the extra point put us up, 10-0.

That was one of my favorite plays of my entire career.

After they scored a touchdown, I responded with one of my own, diving into the end zone to stretch our lead to 17-7.

Later, LSU recovered a fumble. That got the crowd back into it. LSU drove down the field and scored to make it 17-14 after a fake field goal. We kept fighting, though. We scored on a thirty-seven-yard pass to CI (Cornelius Ingram). Now we led 24-14.

Even after they scored to cut our lead to 24-21, we had chances to score. But we didn't. Then with just a minute left to play, they marched down the field and scored.

Talk about a crazed atmosphere.

On the last play, we had time for a Hail Mary, but I overthrew it, just past Coop's hands. LSU hung on to win by a heartbreaking score of 28-24.

The game was ultracompetitive, ultraexciting, and one of my favorites to play in. At the same time, the loss was also devastating to me and to all of us. It was crushing to come so close and do so many things well as a team yet just not do enough to win. We didn't make big mistakes in that game. It was just a series of little things that tripped us up because we weren't focused enough.

We had a week off before we played Kentucky, and during that week, Kentucky beat LSU. We headed to Lexington the weekend of the game. Kentucky hadn't beaten the University of Florida in two decades. And they didn't do it this time, either. The final score was 45-37.

Early in the fourth quarter, I bounced off one of their players as I carried the ball down the field. Off balance, I put my hand on the ground to brace myself, and another player hit me right on the same shoulder. Right away, I could tell that the hit had really damaged it. I couldn't even lift my right arm. Thank goodness, it's my nonthrowing arm.

The next day, I had medical tests on my shoulder. We found out that it was an AC (acromioclavicular joint) separation and a sprain. That was really bad timing since the next week we had to get ready to go play Georgia.

I prayed regularly for my shoulder to heal, a process which was way too slow in coming. I had a few why? moments—not so much "why me?"—but "why not go ahead and heal it now, Lord?" I wondered what lesson

I was supposed to be learning through this—I thought I had gotten a bit better at patience. But the truth of the matter was that as much as I loved the scripture verse from Isaiah, I wasn't always real good at embracing it in my life:

Yet those who wait for the Lord will gain new strength; they will mount up with wings like eagles, they will run and not get tired, they will walk and not become weary.

I get the "mount up with wings like eagles" part—I have felt His power and protection in the midst of some of the most difficult of situations. I get the part about "they will run and not get tired, they will walk and not become weary"; I have felt His hand on my back in moments when I didn't understand what was going on and why.

But I wasn't real good at the "wait for the Lord" part. You would think that when we stop and take a look at all He has done since the beginning of time and throughout the universe—let alone in my life—it would be easy to wait . . . but it isn't.

• • •

Even though I wasn't close to 100 percent, it was exciting to go back to Jacksonville—my home—for the annual battle between Florida and Georgia.

As we were getting ready for Georgia, I could no longer raise my right arm above my head, because of my injury. The coaches came up with a game plan that would allow me to run a little less without keeping me out of the game completely.

I did end up running for a touchdown. My shoulder was killing me. It was tough.

By halftime, I could barely lift my right shoulder at all. Toward the end of the first half, I had been catching snaps with basically just my left hand.

The second half produced one of the worst plays of my college career. With Cornelius Ingram wide open, I missed him. Threw it about three yards over his head. Had I been accurate, it would have gone for at least fifty or sixty yards—maybe a touchdown. Instead, we got nothing on that drive. My fault.

We lost, 42-30.

That game taught us that some of the concerns that showed up as we began spring practice were still with us. Some of the guys were out of shape. Others weren't taking the games seriously enough.

That night after the Florida-Georgia game, I stayed at home on the farm in Jacksonville with my family, and we went out to eat. I take losing hard, but being around my family has always helped put things into the right perspective. Even so, I wasn't very hungry. The next day, I drove back to Gainesville with my brother Peter. It was one of the worst drives back for two reasons: I still couldn't get rid of the sickening feeling I had as a result of the game, how it had happened, and how frustrating it was to endure that 42-30 loss. And then there was my shoulder, which I had reinjured during the game. On both fronts, I was upset and concerned. Things seemed to be heading in the wrong direction for us. We gutted it out, though, and turned our frustrations toward our next opponent.

12

THE HEISMAN

You are the light of the world. A city set on a hill cannot be hidden. —Matthew 5:14 (NASB)

THE FOLLOWING WEEK we played Vanderbilt, who made the mistake of showing up that day. We managed the ball very well.

My coaching career, if I ever have one, started that day. As we huddled on the sidelines, the coaches called the play, but I didn't really like the call.

"How about if we run a naked bootleg and then pass to (wide out) Jarred Fayson?" I suggested. Coach Meyer wasn't sure it would work, but he said he trusted me and to go ahead and go for it. My play worked, so of course, I gave Coach a hard time, telling him, "This coaching stuff isn't that hard. I like this gig."

South Carolina was up next, and ESPN broadcast the Saturday night game. We loved Saturday night television games, except this one turned out to be one of the coldest games I ever played in my college career. Around game time, it was freezing.

Still, there was really good energy in the stadium. The Gamecock fans knew that they had come incredibly close to winning the last time we played. If we hadn't blocked a field goal at the end of that game, we wouldn't have made it to the national championship.

On the opening drive, I scored on a third-down play, and we went up quickly, 7-0. When they got the ball, they turned it back over to us, and I threw a touchdown pass to Jarred Fayson in the corner of the end zone. The score was 14-0.

From that point on, we each took our turns scoring.

When we went into the locker room at halftime, we were up 27-14.

In the fourth quarter on fourth down and goal, I ran it, smashed into two guys on the goal line, and piled over them to get it into the end zone for the touchdown. We knew the game was ours. To end it, we scored another touchdown on a pass that I threw to Bubba Caldwell for a 51-31 win.

After the game, a reporter asked me how it felt to score all those touchdowns. I knew we'd had a big night but didn't realize I'd had a hand in seven touchdowns— five rushing and two passing.

The next week, both our offense and defense continued on a roll and beat Florida Atlantic University. They played us tough but in the end, we won the game.

Before our next game against the Florida State Seminoles, their linebacker Geno Hayes was quoted as saying, "Tim Tebow is going down. We can go out there and shatter his dream." Of course, that comment helped fuel the fire for all of us. My dream, really, was to beat FSU—badly.

On our very first drive, the referee called a false start. We had already started the play, so I continued and went out to my left before they blew the whistle. After they blew it, Geno Hayes slapped me in the face mask, and then head-butted me after we had all clearly stopped.

Not a good idea. At all.

The next play was a third down and sixteen. It was supposed to be a pass play, but nobody was open when I looked around, so I tucked the ball under my arm and ran for a first down. Oh, and during the run I made

FSU's trash-talking, face-mask-slapping, and head-butting linebacker, Geno Hayes, miss.

Although the score was still 0-0, the game was over at that point. After faking a handoff, I stood up, then quickly ducked to avoid a defensive lineman who was coming at me. He flew over my back, and I ran the ball in for a touchdown. As I scored, I thought, *This is going to be a great day.*

That proved to be true when I threw one of my best passes of the year. Running, Louis Murphy caught my throw just as he landed in the back-right corner of the end zone. He did a great job getting a foot down and in the end zone for the score, and we went up 14-3.

In the second quarter, we drove down the field again and ran a "Mickey" up the middle from the five yard line. I stiff-armed a guy in the face mask at the one yard line, with my right hand pressed against his face mask. As I did that, another guy missed me and hit my right hand, pinning it between his and the other player's helmet. I felt something crack as I was getting up and celebrating a new lead with my team, 28-6.

Even with my injured hand, I was able to finish the game, and we dominated it in all aspects, ending up scoring some more and eventually winning, 45-12.

Games against Florida State were big deals to our team. We had played well. For me individually and for the team as a whole, it was a wonderful feeling and a night to enjoy.

After the game, we went to get an X-ray of my hand and found out that it was a complete break. People were surprised to hear I had been playing that way since the second quarter, but nothing was going to keep me from defeating FSU.

Newspapers, magazines, and TV and radio stations were interested in that game for a lot of different reasons. The game against FSU was the last game of the season. Postseason awards were now on everyone's mind in college football, and I was blessed to have been included in the consideration for a number of them. I had to go to Orlando for the Home Depot College Football Awards ceremony, and then on to New York the following day for the Heisman Trophy award ceremony. The Heisman Memorial Trophy award is given to the most outstanding college football player, so it's a great honor to be nominated.

The Heisman Trophy award ceremony was unlike anything I'd experienced before. I'd never been to

New York City, and of course, our whole family went. We received the invitation on Wednesday, and then the Heisman ceremony was on Saturday.

I was excited that my parents, brothers Robby and Peter, sister Katie and her husband Gannon and her daughter Abby, and sister Christy and her husband Joey and her daughter Claire, who are missionaries in Southeast Asia, were all able to attend.

We had a great time there as a family. Immediately after arriving, we gathered as a group, and Dad prayed that we would be able to let our light shine during the ceremony and throughout the weekend, win or lose. By our actions, we could show the world who we really were. It wouldn't have been the same without my entire family. Coach Howard and Coach Mick were there. Coach Meyer had even brought his family. I certainly view them as part of my family as well. Our large, outgoing group enjoyed our time with the other nominees—Colt Brennan, Darren McFadden, Chase Daniel, and their families. They were great.

On Saturday night at a small party before the award presentation ceremony, we were at the Nokia Theatre with twenty-seven players who had won the Heisman Trophy before. We couldn't believe it was real. My dad turned to me and said, "Can you believe that we're even here? And that these guys are actually talking … to us?"

We had so much fun, and right before the ceremony started, former Florida quarterback Danny Wuerffel, who was there as a prior winner, grabbed me, took me into a room in the back, and prayed with me. It was a special moment with someone I respected and had admired since I was young.

It was a thrill for me—for all of us—to win. I'd spent a great deal of time thinking about what I wanted to say, about my family, my university, my coaches and team, and my relationship with God. I received some positive comments from people about my acceptance speech. I don't think they realized how long I'd been practicing— from my mission work in the Philippines to that first public speaking class with Professor Webster at the University of Florida.

We later received a letter from a family who said that their son had accepted Christ after watching my Heisman acceptance speech. That was an incredibly worthwhile moment for me.

The next day, I was signing souvenirs and memorabilia, along with past Heisman winners who were in New

York City for that weekend. We found ourselves alone with Herschel Walker, the University of Georgia's great running back. Spending time with him and listening to him talk about how he ended up playing for Georgia was one of the most memorable times of my college career. He also described some of the highlights of his own long and spectacular college and professional football career.

I won other awards, too. I was a Walter Camp All-American, and I won the Maxwell Award, the first of two ESPYs, and also the Sullivan Award. The Sullivan Award hadn't been won by a football player since Peyton Manning ten years earlier. When I won the O'Brien Award, I got to hang out with Troy Aikman.

Because of my broken hand, I ended up practicing only a little bit for the game against the University of Michigan, the team we would face in the Capital One Bowl in Orlando. But I was still catching balls with my left hand and throwing them back with the same hand in practice.

That year, the bowl organizers had arranged for our entire team to go to a theme park two nights before the game. I wasn't going to go. I still get dizzy on roller coasters, so I figured it was a good night to stay in my room and get some rest. Right before the team left, though, I got a call from Officer Stacy Ettel from the University of Florida Police Department. He always traveled with us to keep us safe. He said the head of the amusement park had been calling for the last hour trying to get me there. Officer Stacy was just passing along the request.

"They just want to meet you," Stacy said. "They also want you to come in so they can actually advertise to the world and say that you're there. That's it."

I have a really hard time turning people down. Depending on the situation, that can either be a good or bad quality. So I quickly got dressed to go to the amusement park, but I knew that if they asked me to get on a ride, I'd tell them I get motion sickness. Once I arrived, they were so excited that I was there that they asked me to please try out their new ride. I looked to Officer Stacy for help, and he tried, but I finally agreed to go for a ride on it. A couple of people from the amusement park went with me. We skipped past all those waiting in line. And we ended up at the front of the line.

Even worse, we were on the front row of the front

car of the new roller coaster—all of which I feared was bound to bring on one of my dizzy spells.

I knew this was going to be bad. Very bad. As we took off, I was gripping the bar tightly. The roller coaster took us up, rolling around and around as it climbed. Over and over, around and around, the new ride went for what had to be the longest roller coaster ride ever. When the ride finally ended, there were folks with cameras, taking pictures, and shouting "Tebow … Tebow … Tebow."

I said anxiously yet as calmly as I could, "Officer Stacy, I'm going to throw up everywhere. The faster you can get me out of here, the better chance the theme-park folks don't see me throwing up all over the place after a trip on their new ride."

As we walked out, I was throwing up behind my clenched teeth until we got around the corner. I couldn't hold it any longer. I got past the end of the line of people and just took off and sprinted about twenty yards until I got behind the nearest building. That's where I began to throw up. I was trying to catch my breath, and my head was spinning like crazy. We stood there for about twenty more minutes, and Officer Stacy kept people away from that corner. It was horrible. The management people came by and apologized for putting me through that, and I politely said, "No, it's okay. It's an unbelievable ride." I'm sure it really would have been fabulous—for anyone but me.

They poured cold water over me. My shirt was soaked, and I was a wreck. I threw up all the way back in the police car. Officer Stacy finally got me back to my hotel room, put me into my bed, and turned out the lights. It was one of the most horrible nights of my life. I just can't do roller coasters, or Ferris wheels, or similar amusement park rides. I can barely do bumper cars.

Meanwhile, my whole family was there for the Capital One Bowl Game. It was a strange one. Michigan had a good game plan and won. The 41-35 loss we suffered was a disappointing way to end our season.

With an ending like that, there was no denying that we had work to do. It had been an up-and-down season in which we beat two of our three archrivals (Tennessee and Florida State), had some great games, and won some great awards. Overall, though, there was a little bit of emptiness and regret because we knew we could have done much better. We knew we left some wins on the field. Now we had a lot of reasons to move into the next off-season with a brand-new motivation to be the best that we could possibly be.

For me, it had been a thrill to win the Heisman and the other awards. But not having a better season as a team diminished the luster. I would continue to work hard, as always, and continue to be a leader for the other guys. And I was hoping it would connect with the guys in 2008 in a way it hadn't in 2007.

13

DOING THE RIGHT THING

For I was hungry, and you fed Me. I was thirsty, and you gave Me a drink. I was a stranger, and you invited Me into your home. I was naked, and you gave Me clothing. I was sick, and you cared for Me. I was in prison, and you visited Me . . . I tell you the truth, when you did it to one of the least of these my brothers, you were doing it to Me! —Matthew 25:35-36, 40 (NLT)

FOR A WHILE, I had been thinking about finding a special way to help kids, but the first time I mentioned it to anyone else was when we were in New York City for the Heisman award ceremony in December 2007. After an official dinner, Zack Higbee and I headed out for more to eat. Zack was a member of Florida's Sports Information Department.

During this time, I had been receiving a number of requests for personal appearances around the

Gainesville area. Arrangements were made for us to visit the hospital on a weekly basis, especially the children's ward. I loved spending time with the kids. I hated that they were going through challenges, but I absolutely admired their spirit. I always came away from those visits encouraged and inspired by their courage.

"I want to use my platform to raise money to help children," I told Zack. He didn't seem surprised. I told him I thought I could raise some money in and around the Gainesville area because of all the folks who knew me there. I was constantly asked to appear at events and sign autographs. Maybe there was a way I could use that popularity to raise money for the orphanage my family started in the Philippines.

I truly believe that the God who loves me also looks at orphans as extremely special. Over and over, my parents showed us how the Bible talks about taking care of widows and orphans. God created each one unique, with gifts and abilities like no one else, for His purposes in this world. Being able to explain that to orphans is an amazing experience, to tell them God's story, like: "The best dad out there—God—loves you so much and wants to adopt you into His family." I've always found this to be the best, most encouraging thing you can tell an orphan, that we're all adopted into the family of God. Follow it up with a long hug, and then a lifetime of caring and commitment so that they have a chance to become all that God created them to be.

Not long after our bowl game against Michigan, Zack and I met with a University of Florida official to find out what the rules were in this situation. We teamed up with some of the sororities, which are women's organizations on campus, to put on a Powder Puff football tournament to raise funds. Powder Puff football games are made up of teams of women. We decided that the money we raised would go to Uncle Dick's Home in the Philippines, as well as a number of local charities. We wanted the students to feel a real connection to what they were doing, and we decided that raising some of the money for local charities they knew about would give them that connection.

We called it *First and 15*, and the tournament was scheduled to follow the Orange and Blue football game in April. We prayed that it wouldn't rain . . . but it did. Still, we had a tremendous time, raising more than $13,000 for the charities. We were pleased, considering it was our first effort. And we learned so much that we knew the event could be even more successful the next year.

Back on the football field, the team that was getting ready for the 2008 season looked a lot different from the 2007 team. Our workouts were crazier, and the competitions within the team were far more intense. In fact, the previous year didn't even begin to compare to what the team was doing in 2008. Not even close. We knew we had a different team.

Simply put, we seemed to have a better, more committed bunch of guys. The whole team began to bond and was working extremely hard individually and together. One February workout was so hard that we called it the Saint Valentine's Day Massacre. It was an immediate bonding experience. And throughout it all, players were saying, "*We're not going to lose in the fourth quarter.*" You could see a change in the team.

We did Midnight Lifts in the summer that were particularly difficult. And, of course, at midnight. The Friday workouts in the off-season were usually the hardest. We also held an annual strength competition that I made sure to win.

Some of the workouts would be linked to how our

partner performed. For instance, Coach Mick would make one guy push a forty-five-pound plate, flat on the floor, around the perimeter of our weight room. And it's a big weight room. Very big. When he began, his partner was seated against the wall as if he is sitting in an invisible chair—with a sandbag on his thighs. The partner against the wall couldn't stop until the partner pushing the forty-five-pound plate had gone all the way around the floor of the weight room. So the partner with the weight wanted to go as fast as he could. One player was responsible for the other.

Responsibility. That would carry over onto the field throughout this season, which at the moment looked like it was going to be very special.

Coach Mick loved those sorts of workouts.

Sometimes when Coach Mick and I were working on our own, he'd be naming off other quarterbacks in college football, saying, "Do one for him . . . do one for him. Do one more for Stafford. Do one more for Bradford. And one more for McCoy."

Those workouts always gave me more confidence. They consisted of exercises I either wouldn't do on my own or wouldn't even consider doing because they hurt so badly. But I would do them for Coach Mick.

And in the process of going beyond where I thought I could go, I started to develop more confidence in my ability to handle whatever I might face—in a game, a classroom, or any other setting. There's no way I would have accomplished the things I've accomplished in my career if I hadn't trained like that and always pushed myself to do something beyond what I'd done before.

It wasn't all work during the spring preparation for the 2008 season. I also had classes, of course, and other stuff. One weekend in the spring, Robby got a call from one of the guys with the country band Rascal Flatts, telling him they'd be in Tampa with singer Darius Rucker and asking if we'd like to come. We had met them when they'd come to Jacksonville for a concert, and we had become friends with them.

Robby was talking with band member Gary LeVox, and I was yelling, "Tell him yes! Darius Rucker is awesome!" In the meantime, Gary was telling Robby that Darius was a fan of mine and was hoping to meet us. So Robby, our friend Bryan Craun, and I headed to Tampa to play golf and meet up with Darius Rucker and Rascal Flatts.

As it turns out, Darius is very competitive on the golf course. Plus, he liked talking about the college he had gone to, the University of South Carolina. We had a good time on a beautiful day, with views looking out over Tampa Bay. That night, we went to the concert and sat on the edge of the stage. Darius pulled me out at one point to join him on a song. Anybody who heard me sing onstage with Kenny Chesney knows that I prefer staying in the background at concerts, but as always, we had a fun night.

A DISCOURAGING START AND A PROMISE

I can do all things through Christ who strengthens me.
—Philippians 4:13 (NKJV)

. . . From everyone who has been given much, much will be required; and to whom they entrusted much, of him they will ask all the more. —Luke 12:48 (NASB)

ALL SUMMER, I kept the workouts going—even when I traveled for mission trips or vacations. My brothers helped me out everywhere we went. I was not about to lose the edge I'd built up with my teammates in the spring. I trained in London, England; Croatia and Bosnia in Eastern Europe; Thailand and the Philippines in Asia; and in the airport terminal in Frankfurt, Germany. Seven countries in three weeks, if you include the United

States. We did exercises with whatever equipment we could find—stairs, chin-up bars, or rough mountain roads. What we used for the workouts didn't matter. What mattered was making sure that I did them.

Even more important than training is having the mindset to want to do it. Coach Mick let me borrow a book called *The Edge*. He keeps reminding me to give it back—I'm sure I will ... one of these days. The book is full of great motivational quotes, like "The Man in the Glass." In this case, a "glass" is a mirror. During a workout, Coach Mick would say, "Are you going to regret what you see in the mirror tonight?" I worked harder.

Coach Mick and I had a really unique relationship. You might think that winning the Heisman meant I could do almost anything I wanted. Instead, I felt that to be worthy as a leader, I had to work twice as hard as everyone else. Coach Mick encouraged that side of me. Then he'd take it even further because that's just the way he'd push me. If I ever made an excuse that I'd already done more than anybody else, he'd say, "Oh, so you only want to be as good as everybody else."

It was hard to tell which one of us was more obsessive.

Working like that gives you such a confidence to be

able to overcome anything you face. You don't care how hard you get hit, because you've already faced harder situations over and over while working out or practicing. By overcoming all those, I knew I was more prepared to overcome whatever I faced. Coach Mick repeated a quote from Michael Jordan about being willing to take a risk:

I've missed more than nine thousand shots in my career. I've lost almost three hundred games. Twenty-six times, I've been trusted to take the game-winning shot and missed. I've failed over and over and over again in my life. And that is why I succeed.

As the Bible says, to whom much is given much is expected. I believe that God wants us to maximize our talents and not hide or waste them. We need to go out there and double them, regardless of whether anyone is watching. It's about going out every day, in every setting, and working hard. It's about being dedicated and playing hard. Whatever you do, do it with all your heart. Because I honestly believe that God receives joy when He sees me using the skills and abilities that He blessed me with.

From the time we were very young, Mom and Dad

would talk to us about sticking up for someone who was being bullied, talking to someone whom no one else would talk to, or befriending a kid who wasn't popular at church. My parents would see us trying to do those things and would reinforce those behaviors by telling us that God will honor that action. Things like encouraging the guys who are down after practice, or talking to a kid who's sick, or making friends with the kids who aren't cool, even though it's not your first reaction. Most of the time you end up having better relationships with those kids and you find out they really are cool.

I find that I get more joy talking to sick children than I could have imagined. Usually, I go visit them because I think I can really help them by spending time with them. But then when I leave, I find myself thinking, *That wasn't the right thing just for* him—*it was the right thing for* me. And I leave better and blessed.

I also worry about people who can't defend themselves or are not really good in sports. They tend to be taken advantage of, mistreated, or bullied. I try to stand up for them since I've always thought that's the right thing to do. That's what my dad always said to us: Try to make others feel how important they are, and find a way to make them feel involved in whatever you and your friends are doing. The message to us was always about doing the right thing. Doing what is right and doing what authority figures ask you to do demonstrates a way of treating other people the way you want to be treated.

By the time fall was upon us, all our preparation was paying off. We had confidence and were ready to start the season—hungrier than we'd been all of last year. We opened the season with Hawaii.

We didn't play particularly well against the Warriors from the Islands, but we still won, 56-10. A few things went wrong: my timing with the receivers, my accuracy, or our connections could have been better. Fortunately, the defense played very well.

I did suffer a setback, however. Early in the game when I went to block, a guy ducked as I lunged to hit him. I'm not sure how it all happened, but I rolled over him onto the ground, and he then ran over my right shoulder, the same one I'd hurt against Kentucky. As a result, I aggravated the injury. I was so mad at myself. I had an AC sprain again, starting from the third play in the 2008 season.

I tried to look past the injury and just focus on our next game: Miami.

Both teams were fired up for this game, and during the pre-game warm-up, I used so much energy that I had to regroup and regather myself to get a second wind. Maybe it was because of this excitement or maybe it was just the mood I was in; the Miami game was the first time I ever wrote a Bible verse beneath my eyes. I was getting ready to put on eye black before the game and trying to decide whether to wear the black paint stuff or the black patches that are like stickers. I thought maybe I could use a Sharpie to write a Bible verse on the eye black if I used the patches—I figured that black paint would just make a total mess.

I wasn't even sure if people would be able to see it, but I thought if they could, it might be a really simple way to share a great Bible verse with some folks in the television-viewing audience. And if somebody noticed and asked me about it, I'd have a chance to talk about things of real significance beyond football.

The first verse that came to mind was one of my favorites, Philippians 4:13:

I can do all things through Christ who strengthens me.

That was perfect to summarize my approach to football, and it seemed like a good verse to go with the first time out of the box. Paul's point is that Christ gives us the ability to be content with a little or a lot.

I wrote it on the eye-black patches and wore the patches into the game. I don't remember that it got a lot of attention, and I really hadn't given any thought to whether I would do it again. As I recall, a few reporters asked me about it after the game. And so I continued to write Philippians 4:13 on the eye-black patches all through the rest of the season. Actually, I wrote "PHIL" under my right eye and "4:13" under my left. Occasionally I'd have someone ask who Phil was and what that number had to do with him. And even that question gave me a chance to talk about things of eternal significance.

Early in the game, I threw to Aaron Hernandez in the corner of the end zone for a touchdown. But it was all uphill from there, a tough game. Miami made some big plays and kept it somewhat close, but we played pretty well and managed to stay ahead, largely due to Aaron, who had a great game.

Because it was early in the season, we were still getting used to who was doing what. In the off-season, we never fully know who our playmakers will be and who will emerge as key players. A few guys stepped up when we needed them, making some big plays and demonstrating leadership and passion.

Miami was a big win for us. Because it was the only time I'd get to play against them, I certainly didn't want to miss this opportunity to beat them. I wanted to make certain we did everything we needed to do to end up with a victory. The defense played well once again, holding Miami to only three points. Our 26-3 win was a total team effort—we scored early and finished up by scoring late.

The next week, we played Tennessee in Knoxville. The year before, we'd beaten them pretty badly in the Swamp, so we knew they were going to come in motivated to turn that around. Still, they were the ones who won the SEC East Division the previous year, not us. We drove down the field and scored on our first possession of the game on a pass to Aaron Hernandez. We led 20-0 at the half. Tennessee's only points came in the second half, and we won, 30-6. It's always good to win an SEC game, but it's particularly big when you can go to Neyland Stadium in Knoxville with their 110,000 fans and come away with a big win.

We had gotten through a tough early stretch and thankfully had a bit of a breather ahead, with Ole Miss coming into the Swamp.

In the history of playing against Ole Miss, Florida had lost only one more game than they had. We would tie it with a win. But more important than any history, a victory would make us 2-0 in the conference for 2008. We were starting to play pretty well on offense, and we were hoping to match the defense's continuing high level of play in this week's game.

However, for some reason, we seemed to be kind of down the whole game. It's hard to even explain. We started out fine—moved the ball fairly well, scored some points, and went up 17-7 at halftime. Usually, there'd be a point in the second quarter where the players' internal switches would flip on like a light. We'd automatically feel some additional drive, get the momentum, and score a touchdown. Or the defense would stop them, and then we'd begin to dominate them. But in the Ole Miss game, we never felt that click or anything similar. Several times, I thought we'd start blowing them out, because we really were better than they were.

Honestly, it's hard to even explain some of the things that happened in that game.

In the second quarter, we ran a shovel pass, a sideways underhand toss. It turned out to be a great call by the coaches. It caught Ole Miss off guard. But after his catch and run for a thirty-yard gain, Aaron Hernandez fumbled—our first turnover of the year. Later, I fumbled a handoff to Brandon James when we both let go of the ball, and it fell to the ground. Their defensive end recovered the dropped ball on our own eighteen yard line. That was the only time I fumbled on a handoff exchange in my entire career at Florida.

We knew we were so much better than they were, but we weren't playing like it. Usually, we found a way to win, but we struggled to find one that day. Near the end of the game, they scored on a long touchdown pass to go up 31-24. The Swamp was silent.

We got the ball back, and I felt that there was no chance they would stop us now. I was right. We drove the ball right down the field for the tying touchdown, but the extra point that we needed for the tie was blocked. The score was 31-30.

We got the ball back again with only a little bit of time left. We started out strong with some successful passing, then when things seemed to be going great, we missed a couple of passes. Then on a third-down play, we came up just short, and it was fourth and one from their thirty-two yard line.

It was the ball game at that moment. A field goal would have been a forty-nine-yard attempt. Instead, Coach called my number on a short yardage play to get the first down. Unfortunately for us, Ole Miss made a great call. Instead of blitzing straight down the middle, they blitzed off to the right side, where we were making our play. Even the cornerback blitzed off the edge of the defense, a very unusual move that surprised us.

There might have been three or four times in my four years that I was stopped on a short-yardage play. Unfortunately, that was one of them.

To this day, I still don't think that team should've beaten us or taken our undefeated season from us. And certainly not at home in the Swamp.

Going into that game, we felt like we controlled our destiny, but when we arrived, we simply weren't mentally or emotionally prepared—any of us. I can't explain it, but I can tell you that because of my position and role on the team, I felt largely responsible for our loss.

Walking off the field, I couldn't believe we'd lost.

The coaches' goal was to win the SEC East and play in the SEC Championship Game, but for us players . . . we also wanted an undefeated season. It had never happened at Florida. That was now gone. We might still be able to win the SEC East, or even the national championship, but we had a loss.

Coach Meyer's comments to us afterward were positive, but I was struggling with the loss. The players got dressed.

I sat alone in my locker for about forty-five minutes, replaying the game over and over in my head. This wasn't supposed to have happened. We had spent so many hours over the summer working and training on our own and then with the coaches in the August heat. We worked hard because we wanted to accomplish something that no Florida team had ever accomplished: a perfect season. Now, with an awful second half against a determined Ole Miss team, that undefeated season wasn't going to happen.

UF's Sports Information Department folks kept coming in to ask if I was ready to face the media. Coach Meyer sat right in front of me with his back to me and leaned back against my knee. We sat quietly for quite a while and barely spoke. I knew the media was waiting.

I was still crying off and on, and when I thought that I'd finally pulled myself together enough to face the press, I broke down again. I sat there while Coach gave me a hug, doing his best to make me feel better.

Frustrated doesn't begin to capture how I felt, although that was part of it. I felt betrayed by my teammates, because they hadn't played at a high-enough level.

The more I thought about it, however, the feeling of betrayal faded. The problem lay with me, not them. They had all played hard, but it hadn't been enough. The only thing I could ever control was me and my effort, and I decided that I had been the one who let us down. I took a few minutes to gather my thoughts, and then I got up and began to head out of the locker room with Coach Meyer to face the media.

In my mind, I wasn't going to make a big deal about this press conference. I simply felt embarrassed and ashamed because I felt I'd personally let the Gator Nation down. I wanted to make a little apology to the fans. So I thought about how I wanted to apologize for the lack of enough effort on my part and to promise that they would see a better effort from me for the rest of the year. Finally, when Coach had calmed me down enough to go to the press conference, my parents walked into the locker room and I got emotional again . . . so we had to start the process over while Zack Higbee updated the patiently awaiting questioners that it would just be . . . another . . . minute or two.

Finally, I was all set, although I really didn't want to face the press or anyone else after that particular game.

As I started to apologize, I got a bit emotional in my remarks. Then I got fired up, because that's how I tend to get when I'm speaking. Very passionate. I had given it some thought in the locker room, but it was still pretty much off the cuff and right from the heart:

To the fans and everybody in Gator Nation, I'm sorry. I'm extremely sorry. We were hoping for an undefeated season. That was my goal, something Florida has never done here.

I promise you one thing, a lot of good will come out of this. You will never see any player in the entire country play as hard as I will play the rest of the season. You will never see someone push the rest of the team as hard as I will push everybody the rest of the season.

You will never see a team play harder than we will the rest of the season. God bless.

It wasn't long before they started playing my speech on ESPN *SportsCenter.* My family told me it was good; it was me down deep inside. I do remember having a few of the reporters looking at me like I was crazy. My family and I got in the elevator to go to Coach Meyer's office, and I was covered up in the back of the elevator, hiding, because I didn't want anyone to notice me that day.

One reporter in the front of the elevator turned to another writer next to him and said, "Holy cow. How about that? I know he's for real, but I wonder how the public's going to take that. I think the public will kill him for that."

Those were the first comments I heard, and I cringed listening to them.

By that night, however, the feedback I was getting was all positive. I think that people agreed with the reporter's assessment—I was being sincere. I received a lot of calls and texts that night from people who said they appreciated it and they're supporting me. I have always appreciated the Gator Nation. I certainly did that night. They came through again when I—and my teammates—seemed to need it most.

Soon, I couldn't go anywhere without seeing my words posted on a television screen or somewhere else. For the next few days, I didn't enjoy all the attention my remarks received.

The next day, Coach let me address the team. My comments to my teammates were similar but more intense and personal. In essence, I told them I wasn't asking them to do anything that I wasn't also going to ask myself to do—that I would be the hardest worker in the country the rest of the season and our team would be as well, if they were willing. Nothing was over. We still had a shot to reach our other goals.

Coach Meyer later told me that receiver David Nelson went to his office after that meeting and told him that he wanted to do whatever he could to contribute to this team in any way he could.

David and I weren't the only ones. That loss affected everyone in different ways. But I could see that there was a fire in everybody's eyes and that things would definitely be different. It brought everybody together in a way I had never seen before. I felt, after that, that everyone was now united with one mission and one goal, not to win the conference or the next game, but rather to win the next play. Then the next. We were going to dominate our opponents every step of the game—physically and through our preparation and passion.

From that point forward, as a team, we weren't thinking in terms of being a great offense or defense. Instead, our focus was winning by using our preparation, ability, and determination—one play at a time. Anyone who stood in our way had better watch out.

As always, our signs in the locker room still read, "Get to Atlanta." "<u>47</u> days to Atlanta." Each day the sign was updated: "<u>46</u> days to Atlanta . . ."

We had a great week of practice to get ready for Arkansas on the road and started off the game that day in Fayetteville with a great first drive. By halftime, we had a 14-0 lead.

In the second half, we were leading 17-7, when I hesitated on a throw to Percy Harvin. I threw it too late *and* right into the hands of an Arkansas linebacker. I stepped back as I released the ball and somehow bent my right knee the wrong way.

By the time I got back to the sideline, I was hurting

and furious with myself. Later, we ended up going ahead, 24-7, but I was so mad at myself that I turned and walked off the field. When I looked at Coach Meyer, I could see he was both frustrated and disappointed in my angry attitude. He was looking at me with his hands in the air and mouthing, "Let's go!" and "Get excited!"

I went over to Coach and chest-bumped him, hoping that might snap me out of my mood. Unfortunately, I hit him hard in the mouth with my shoulder pads and chipped his tooth.

Coach wouldn't talk to me for ten minutes because he was mad, and I was mad at myself for playing so badly. Finally, he came over to me and apologized and said he loved me. I said the same thing to him. He smiled—you could see the chipped tooth.

We ended up winning the game, which did help to calm me down some. But I knew that if I was to keep my word after the Ole Miss game, I would have to be better.

We had a good week of practice preparing to host LSU in Gainesville. I worked on making my knee better, and Coach Meyer got his tooth fixed. I was excited all day before the game, and the atmosphere in the Swamp helped to keep me fired up. It was a matchup of the national champions. (We had won it all in 2006, and they won in 2007.)

Early in the game, I threw the ball to Percy, who ran it in for the touchdown. Seventy yards. A perfect way to start the game. From that point on, the whole game went well. I made a lot of good decisions, and threw the ball accurately, making the right calls at the line. I felt that was one of my better games in college.

We won, 51-21. That was a big win for us after losing to them the year before. It kept us on track and made us feel as though we really could keep our promise to one another to play our best.

The week after LSU, we played the University of Kentucky. We blocked their first two punts and scored after each. Then we scored again, blocked their field-goal attempt, and scored again. It was 28-0 at the end of the first quarter.

Once again, we were focused on winning every play. It worked. Final score: 63-5.

We had now played three games after the Ole Miss game and had easily won all three. Clearly, our focus was good. We hadn't expected to score that many points against Kentucky, and we didn't mean to embarrass them. In fact, if we really wanted to embarrass a team, it would have been our opponents the next week—Georgia.

I was probably more nervous about the 2008 Georgia game than I had been in any other game that year. Our loss the year before had been embarrassing, and I wanted to make it up to our fans and the team. More than anything, I wanted to win it for Coach Meyer, because I knew how hurt he had been. I wasn't going to let that happen again. Not to him, not to our team, not to Gator fans.

It started close. We took a 7-0 lead, then they kicked a field goal. After scoring another touchdown, we were up 14-3. We continued to play with focus and passion. We were more physical and simply outplayed them.

With very little time left in the game, we were ahead 49-10. Coach had taken me out of the game, so I ran straight to our fans in the corner of the field and celebrated with them. I was pretty emotional, which fired up the fans even more. The stadium was ordinarily half orange-and-blue and half red-and-black. Now it was mostly orange, blue, and teal, which was the color of all the empty seats. Most of the Georgia fans left with the score in our favor.

It was one of the most exciting times of my life. Period. There we were, in Jacksonville where I grew up. Georgia had embarrassed us the previous year, but on this day, we were beating them up. We obviously wanted it more than they did.

We were playing well, and it was hard to imagine that we'd actually lost a game. The loss against Ole Miss kept driving us to try and dominate every team and every individual that we played. We didn't know how the year would finish, but one game at a time, we were claiming the title of the best team in the country.

The next weekend, we played in Nashville against Vanderbilt. It was early November and we were on a roll.

I played a part in scoring five touchdowns, then Coach took me out, and Johnny Brantley played the fourth quarter. We clinched the SEC East and a trip to the SEC Championship Game with a 42-14 win that cold night in Nashville.

South Carolina was next, and ranked in the top twenty-five. They had a good defense, so we needed to be as prepared as we'd been for the other teams. During my free time, I headed down to the coaches' offices and often sat in on staff meetings as the coaches discussed the plans for the game. The more I knew about a given game plan, the better I felt.

I had done that throughout my time at Florida, meeting individually with the coaches and attending whatever game-planning meetings I could. The more I was around to hear their thinking and watch film, the better prepared I would be for whatever might happen on Saturday.

I owed that to myself and my teammates. If I was going to lead the way I wanted to lead, I needed to be as ready as possible. Therefore, whenever I could fit it in between classes, studying, and tutoring sessions, I did.

We had nearly lost to South Carolina in Gainesville during the national championship season of 2006, so we knew we needed to stay focused during this game. Instead, our offense had a little trouble getting going. Our defense scored our first touchdown on an interception, then Ahmad Black gave us good field position with an interception of his own.

We fumbled twice in the first half but still led, 28-3, at the halftime break. As always with South Carolina, it was a physical game. South Carolina teams always hit. Hard.

We played better in the second half, and like the rest of our games during that period, it wasn't close.

We had two more games left in the regular season: the Citadel, which we won, and then we faced FSU. This time, it was in Tallahassee. A pouring rain soaked the field, and I got garnet paint on my uniform and face early in the game. It ended up looking like blood.

We scored early and often, and as in other Florida State games, I wanted to make contact with someone on each of my runs. Early on, I ran over their safety, and that move helped to set the tone for our approach to the rest of the game. Our guys didn't need any help, however. Percy scored again, and I threw three touchdown passes and ran for another. I even recovered a fumble. We stayed in control all day long.

My one rushing touchdown came after Percy was injured. In every other stadium I've played in, the fans get silent when a player is injured. It doesn't matter if he plays for the home or visiting team. But when Percy went down in front of their stands, the FSU fans burst into loud cheering and chanting. Even before anyone knew if he was all right.

I was angry about the cheering. I jogged over to Coach Meyer.

"Give me the ball."

He nodded.

I hit the line. I stayed up as a couple of FSU defenders tried to tackle me. Most of my teammates joined the pile and pushed me—and the surrounding FSU players—into the end zone. Touchdown.

I ran over to the section of the stands where our fans were seated and waved my arms, getting them really worked up. Throughout the game, we controlled FSU, scoring five of the first seven times we had the ball. And we had more than twice as many yards as they did for the game.

15

A PROMISE FULFILLED

For God loved the world so much that He gave His one and only Son, so that everyone who believes in Him will not perish but have eternal life. —John 3:16 (NLT)

IT WAS A GOOD THING I loved big games, because the week after the FSU game, we had another big one. We were headed to Atlanta for the Southeastern Conference Championship Game against Alabama.

After the 2007 season, Nick Saban had left the Miami Dolphins to replace Mike Shula, and Alabama was playing very well. They were undefeated and ranked number one in the nation. We were ranked number two and had that one loss to Ole Miss, of course. It had been two months since we'd lost, however, and we were a very confident group.

After wearing Philippians 4:13 on my eye black

all season, I thought about switching it for that game and going with John 3:16. I mulled it over for a while but decided to leave it the same. If we ended up on a bigger stage—the BCS National Championship Game for example—I'd switch. The atmosphere was electric in the Georgia Dome. My whole family was there. It was one of those well-played games by both teams, where you're happy to be a part of it. We went into halftime leading 17-10, after David Nelson caught a touchdown pass right before the end of the half. Alabama tied the score on a touchdown then added a field goal to take the lead, 20-17, entering the fourth quarter.

We were both playing for everything—the SEC title and a spot in the national championship game.

We began an offensive drive that was the biggest drive of the game for us. If we didn't score, we knew they might and make it impossible for us to catch up. It was a slow drive where we kept making play after play after play. Great offense versus great defense.

I looked at the faces in the huddle. "We are going to win this game *right now*." I believed. They believed.

We were able to make some great plays and manage the ball. We had the ball on their one yard line, and

Coach Mullen made a great play call. After I flipped the ball to Jeff Demps, he basically walked into the end zone untouched, because our guys made some great blocks.

Great call. Great playing.

We now led again, 24–20, and desperately needed to keep the momentum. I ran over and head-butted everybody on the kickoff team. I hoped it would get them all fired up. I don't really know if the head butts were the reason or not, but our kickoff team and defense made some key defensive plays to stop Alabama. We got the ball back with just a few minutes left to play.

The only way we were going to be safe was if we scored a touchdown. If we kicked a field goal, we would still only be winning by seven points and they could tie us on a single play. With a touchdown, they would need to score twice.

We kept moving the ball down the field. Eventually, we had a first down from their twenty-one yard line. I threw a shovel pass to Aaron Hernandez and got the first down. It was a huge call.

On first and goal, I ran the ball and gained five yards. Second and goal from the one.

Flag. A yellow flag was down on the field. The

officials called a penalty on Coach Meyer for being too far on the field. I've never seen something like that.

Now we were on the six yard line with second down and goal to go for a touchdown. We desperately needed a touchdown.

Our coaches called Trick Left 51 X Stutter Bend Cash. Riley Cooper was supposed to run from the right toward the middle of the field. I knew that Alabama's defense would be trying to figure out the play by looking at my eyes. After the snap, I immediately looked left and saw a linebacker and a safety reading my eyes. I quickly threw right to Coop. I had to throw it down and in front of Coop, because of the defenders' positions. He did the rest. That was one of the biggest plays of Riley's and my career.

That was the game right there. We had so much momentum. Our defense kept them from scoring, and we ran out the clock. We were the SEC champions and would be playing in the national championship game in South Florida early in January 2009.

Afterward, Coach Meyer said he thought my performance was the best fourth-quarter performance that he's ever seen from a player. All I know is, it felt good to help the team and get us to the next game. The victory belonged to everyone that day. A whole lot of us contributed to keeping the promise we had made to one another.

The next morning, however, my head was killing me. At first, I didn't understand why. Then I looked in the mirror and saw the knots all over my forehead. That's when I realized what I'd done. Those head butts with the kickoff team? I'd forgotten that I didn't have my helmet on. I'll never do that again.

While we were beginning our practices for Oklahoma in the national championship game later that month, I went to my second Heisman Trophy award ceremony as a finalist. I was really hopeful about being a two-time winner of the Heisman.

Unfortunately, this time I didn't win. But that only made my desire stronger. I'd been to the BCS Championship once, and now I was headed back. And I was determined to win.

Game on.

We had a month to prepare. I have never been more nervous than I was headed into the BCS National Championship Game. The fact that it was my second one didn't change a thing. We were playing Oklahoma, and "game on" or not, they were really good. They were the highest scoring team in college football history and had scored more than *sixty* points five games in a row.

But if there was any defense that could handle them, it was our defense. Hands down. And they would be ready.

Thursday afternoon before the game, I decided to have a last-minute Bible study. I called as many guys as could fit into our hotel room. I felt led to talk about Matthew 11:28-30, which says,

Come to me, all who are weary and heavy-laden, and I will give you rest.
Take My yoke upon you and learn from Me, for I am gentle and humble in heart, and you will find rest for your souls. For My yoke is easy and My burden is light.

I told my teammates gathered that Jesus promises to take on the weight of the world, so that we don't have to. All we needed to do was follow Him.

I then looked around the room and said, "Guys, we are going to win the National Championship tonight. And when we do, we are going to give so much honor and glory to Jesus Christ. It is going to be awesome."

Somebody had a guitar, and for the next couple of hours, we just sang hymns and other worship songs. There were a lot of bad voices in that room, but none of us cared. The Bible says to "make a joyful noise to the Lord" (see Psalm 98:4), but it doesn't say anything about a "good" noise—thankfully.

Before the game that night, I walked up to Coach Meyer and told him that I had prayed about it, and that I was going to change the scripture on my eye black to John 3:16.

"You can't. What are you thinking?" was his immediate response. "Philippians 4:13 is such a *great* verse," he continued. We both knew that it was the same superstitious streak bubbling up in him that caused him to sit on the forty-fifth row at Florida Field three years earlier when waiting for my announcement.

I repeated that I was changing it to John 3:16. He looked into my eyes and could tell that I knew it was the right thing to do. He paused. "Yeah, that's a great one, too. Okay, that'll be *great*!" And, excited about it, he bounded onto the bus.

After getting dressed in my uniform, I passed Coach Mullen in the locker room, and he immediately noticed the change.

"What's that verse about?" he asked.

"'For God so loved the world, that He gave His only begotten Son, that whoever believes in Him shall not perish, but have eternal life,'" I replied.

His jaw dropped. "Can you do that with *every* verse in the Bible? I just name one, and you quote it?"

I laughed. "Unfortunately, no." Thanks to my parents, I had memorized a lot in my life, but not all of them. Of course, I stacked the deck—I made sure that I knew the ones I was writing under my eyes.

Neither team scored in the first quarter. I threw an interception early in the game, which was disappointing since I had thrown only two all year.

In the second quarter, we jumped to an early lead— 7-0. Oklahoma quickly tied the score at 7-7, and then they intercepted my pass. We paid them back by picking off a pass from their quarterback, Sam Bradford. The two teams had led the nation in fewest turnovers during the season. Together we now had three in the first half. It was 7-7 at halftime.

Game on.

It was time for all of those hours, days, and months in the weight room to pay off. And it did.

Early in the third quarter, we took the lead, 14-7.

Oklahoma tied it, then we took the lead again with a field goal—17-14.

In the fourth quarter, Ahmad Black picked off Sam Bradford. We needed a big lead to ensure a win.

I threw a jump pass to David Nelson. He caught it and scored the touchdown that put the game away, 24-14.

Moments later, we had the ball back. As we were running out the clock, I thought an Oklahoma player gave me an extra jab in the pile. I scrambled up and gave him a Gator Chomp with my arms. The referee called a penalty. It was the only unsportsmanlike conduct penalty of my career. I shouldn't have done it.

Game over. We were the national champions!

After the final touchdown I walked over to Coach Meyer. He pulled off his headset, opened up his arms, gave me a great big hug, and said, "Atta boy. Great job. You finished. I love you." It was a great feeling to hear him say that. After all, he had been not only a coach but also a friend and a father figure to me.

As great as that was, how much greater will it feel when we get to heaven and Jesus takes off His headset, opens up His arms, gives us a big hug, and says, "Atta boy. Great job. You finished. I love you."

• • •

I talk to kids all the time about finishing strong. Some people are going to quit, and some people are going to start going slower. But the people who can finish are the ones who are going to succeed. Those are the ones who are going to be great.

When I leave this world, I want to leave something behind that keeps on making a difference in people's lives.

In addition to living by this motto myself, I talk to prison inmates about it. I started visiting prisons my freshman year and have been to quite a few, even visiting death row. I really enjoy speaking with those guys—they are so hungry for people to interact with them and share anything at all that is encouraging. I tell them that they might have had a bad first, second, or third quarter, but they can still have a great fourth quarter. They can finish strong in life—wherever they are—and it starts by having a personal relationship with Jesus.

For me, leaving something behind is more about being rewarded in heaven. Seeing a plaque or trophy with my name on it sure is nice. But God wants us to make a difference in the world—in the lives of our family, friends, coaches, and teachers. The most important acts will live on forever—even after we are no longer on the earth. He wants us to do things that will last. That's why building a school or a playroom in a hospital is going to leave a legacy with real meaning, not just a name on a plaque or a stadium.

I want to leave behind a life in which I always tried to do things the right way. Most importantly, I want to act in a way that causes the people I help to want to help others. Finish strong and you help not just yourself—you help others.

16

MATCHING THEIR INTENSITY

No, dear brothers and sisters, I have not achieved it, but I focus on this one thing: forgetting the past and looking forward to what lies ahead, I press on to reach the end of the race and receive the heavenly prize for which God, through Christ Jesus, is calling us.
—Philippians 3:13-14 (NLT)

I THOUGHT I'D HAVE a chance to finish strong in college. Since I'd always preached about finishing strong, I wanted to act on what I'd said. Some people thought I should go pro after my junior year. (Once a college player has been in college for three years, he can play with the NFL if a team chooses him.) By leaving college early, I wouldn't have to worry about getting a serious injury in my senior year—before I had a chance to play in the pros.

But there were risks to leaving college, too. If I left, I'd have no chance to be a part of one of the greatest college teams of all time. We could possibly win a third national championship.

I really didn't want to leave Coach Meyer. He and I had become more like brothers than simply coach and player. He and I had lunch together in his office almost every day during the season, just talking. In the end, that relationship was a big part of my decision.

Although I had thought about it and prayed about it a great deal, Coach Meyer and I hadn't spoken a word about my decision. Then, we had a meeting the day after we returned from the national championship game.

It was Coach, my parents, and me. We talked and went through all the pros and cons of the decision. Coach made it clear that he wanted me to stay for selfish reasons. He liked coaching me and hanging out in his office with me. He also thought that if I played one more season, my career might go down as one of the best in college history. I wasn't sure about that, but I agreed that I loved my time with Coach and at Florida.

For me, it was all about finishing strong. I had to do what I had told others to do. I felt that I wanted to finish college strong, to do the best I could, and to be there for my teammates and Coach Meyer. To have a great senior year.

Once I'd decided to stay, I turned my attention to the season.

The coaches wouldn't say it, but our goal as the class of 2009 was to become the best team college football had ever seen. That kept us motivated.

Meanwhile, I continued to try and use my success for other purposes. I organized the First and 15 event once again, but this time we made it a week-long event. We still held the Powder Puff game, but we added a number of other events to make it a full week. We held something we called a Brighter Day Event. Thanks to Bill Heavener, a family friend, we took twelve disadvantaged kids with us to Disney World for the day. One of my favorite events of the week was an ice-cream social in the children's wing at Shands Hospital, with balloons and ice cream in the kids' party room. I always try to eat well, but I really love ice cream. An event with ice cream *and* kids is definitely an event I can look forward to—every year, or even more often.

First and 15 also had an auction. The paint-splattered jersey I wore when we played FSU sold for $250,000.

We raised over $500,000. Part of the money went to add a new children's room at Shands, called *Timmy's Playroom*. In fact, we raised more in one week than any student organization in the country had ever raised.

Every year at the end of July, we'd have a strongman competition at Florida for fans. During that strongman competition, I was flipping tires down the field with Brandon Spikes, my partner. I hadn't stretched out and warmed up very well. I'm not sure what happened, but I tried to pull up with all my might to lift the tire. Instantly, I felt a pain in my lower back. I can be pretty silly sometimes because I'm so competitive, and since the competition was still going on, I didn't stop. I kept going through the pain.

Fortunately, I hadn't done much real damage, but I ended up having to rest at the beginning of training camp that August. When I finally was able to start practicing, I wasn't allowed to engage in any contact. I was getting better each day until I was carrying out a fake and didn't even have the ball. Not thinking, a teammate pushed me from the side. I aggravated my back again and had to sit out even more practices. That loss of practice time due to my back strain bothered me a bit, but it finally cleared up over time.

We opened the year with wins over Charleston Southern and Troy.

Things seemed to be headed in the right direction, but it was hard to tell. Neither of our first two opponents was as good as the teams that were to follow.

Tennessee coach Lane Kiffin seemed to have a lot to say when he brought the Volunteers to play us the following week. In person, he's actually very nice, but in the weeks before the game, he said way too many things to the press about Coach Meyer and the rest of us.

All that talk made the game very emotional. It was also a frustrating game. Early on in the game, I threw the ball poorly and Tennessee intercepted it. Still, we were leading 13-6 at the half and then had a chance to separate ourselves in the second half. We were up 23-6, and then I had a really good run down the right sideline, broke free from the tackler, and was down around the two yard line where I spun and was stripped of the ball. Fumble. Recovered by Tennessee.

Tennessee drove down and scored, making it 23-13. Fortunately, the defense held them for the remainder of the game, and that was the final score, giving us the win.

It was turning into a strange season. We put a lot of pressure on ourselves to achieve something special. We were 3-0 and had won thirteen straight games over the last two seasons, the longest streak in the country . . . but we were miserable. Simply winning didn't seem to be enough to satisfy us.

Looking back, I think we maybe should have enjoyed the 2008 national championship longer than we did. During the off-season, we immediately put pressure on ourselves to succeed. Some guys didn't respond well to that. Certainly, we should have worked hard, but I think we may have overdone it. Even though we were winning, it simply wasn't a very good situation.

With Kentucky up next, we tried to find that drive that had given us so much success the previous year. Unfortunately, my health turned out to be the story of the next week. Make that the next three weeks.

It started on Thursday when I came down with the H1N1 virus, which was better known as swine flu. It came on fast and was awful. I threw up all night. They kept me and the other players who were sick away from the rest of the team because the virus was so contagious. The sick players on our team even had to fly separately from the rest of the team before the game.

By game time, I felt much better. Still, throughout the game, I had to have fluids shot directly into my veins through a needle. The game started off well. Just like most of our games against Kentucky over the last two decades, we dominated them. And I was having a big day running, in spite of the flu.

At one point in the third quarter, we broke from the huddle. I went into my count and caught the snap. I looked for my receiver. *This* play would be a touchdown.

Then darkness.

Next, I saw my parents looking serious, with a low metal ceiling above their heads.

Then darkness.

"It's okay, Timmy," Kyle, our assistant trainer, said. "Just roll over." I couldn't figure out why I was rolling over or what the white metal was around me. I didn't know I was in a hospital, having a test done.

"They're just gonna slide you in there for a CAT scan." I rolled, stayed quiet, and waited for an explanation of why I was there.

• • •

I soon found out what happened. As I was waiting for the receiver to come open, a Kentucky defender had flown into me, hitting me below the chin. I had a concussion—an injury to the brain. That blow wasn't what caused my concussion, though. That happened when the back of my head hit my offensive lineman in the knee as I fell backward.

My family, watching this all unfold from the stands, was horrified. As they always do in times good and bad, they started to pray.

I threw up as I was taken off in a cart. My parents rode in the back of the ambulance to the hospital, concerned and praying as I was checked out.

Coach Meyer told me that my first question when I briefly awoke on the field was, "Did I hold on to the ball?" I did. And my second, in the hospital, was, "Did we win?" We did. Of course, I hated that I hadn't finished the game alongside my teammates, but I was pleased they had gone on to win.

The medical staff kept me up all night, not letting me fall asleep. That's important when someone has had a concussion. They took really good care of me. The next day, I checked out fine and returned to Gainesville.

Thank goodness, we had the week off following the Kentucky game, because our next game was in Baton Rouge against Louisiana. We were ranked number one, and they were ranked number four. Despite our loss there in 2007, I loved playing in Tiger Stadium.

It was a great return to Baton Rouge. We won, 13-3.

The game against Arkansas at our place the following week was remarkable. Arkansas played well, and it was a game to remember. We had an unusual number of fumbles and missed tackles for us, and we were trailing until late in the game.

Still, we tied the game in the fourth quarter at twenty. I felt that it was time for the offense to step up. After all, we had turned the ball over an unacceptable four times. I told Coach to give me the ball—I was in one of those crazy moods.

On a third and ten play, Coop tripped coming off the line. He scrambled up and then caught my pass in the chest for a first down. A huge play. The pass was at chest level because he was going to the ground again. He actually made the catch while on a knee—an amazing grab.

At the end of our drive, Caleb Sturgis kicked a field

goal to win it with nine seconds left. I didn't open my eyes until I heard the crowd roar: 23-20.

Sure, it shouldn't have been that close, but it was a fun game. We had to find a way to win that game, and we did. I was proud of our team.

17

FINISHING STRONG

I have fought the good fight, I have finished the race, I have kept the faith. –2 Timothy 4:7 (NKJV)

I KNEW MISSISSIPPI STATE would be interesting. We were looking forward to seeing Coach Mullen, who had left Florida to coach at Mississippi State. But Coach Mullen knew our strengths and weaknesses, and his game plan definitely proved it.

The game started off well. In the second quarter, I rushed for a touchdown to tie Herschel Walker for the all-time SEC rushing touchdown record. But things went downhill from there. We were ahead 13-3 right before halftime. Then Mississippi State intercepted my pass and ran it back one hundred yards for a touchdown, making it 13-10 at halftime.

Finally, in the fourth quarter, we scored a touchdown to put us up by nine and give us some breathing room. But on Mississippi State's next possession, we intercepted for a touchdown. I'm thankful that we did, because I then threw another interception and they scored a touchdown. Coach Mullen definitely knew how to play against me that night.

We ended up winning, but it wasn't a good feeling for anybody. Afterward, my family gathered around me, under the stadium, helping me deal with it all.

From the outer edges of our group, I could hear somebody asking to get through to me—Dan Mullen. He was great. He took me aside, put his arm around me, and encouraged me. It was a moment I'll never forget.

There was no denying that it had become a surprisingly tough season. I think that because we had such a high standard to be the best ever, we put unnecessary pressure on ourselves rather than just going out and playing the game. What we really needed to do was focus on doing whatever we could to get ready to win games.

We pushed ahead and got ready for our annual skirmish in Jacksonville. Even though they had a lot of good players, Georgia wasn't as good as the year before. I threw two touchdown passes in the first quarter. Then I rushed for a touchdown in the second, breaking former Georgia Heisman Trophy winner Herschel Walker's all-time SEC rushing touchdown mark. To do that against Georgia in my hometown made it that much better. I kept that ball and gave it to my dad for Christmas.

After a first half like that, we knew we were in control, and we went on to beat them handily, 41-17.

The following game was against Vanderbilt. We hoped that we could repeat our solid victory over them from the previous year. We did and beat them by a score of 27-3.

The next game was at South Carolina, and it was tough, as always. I was pleased that we were able to make that game one of the best games of the year, which we won 24-14.

FSU was coming to town for my last game in the Swamp. It was an emotional week.

By pre-game warm-up time, I was throwing the football badly. Was my poor performance because I was so emotional? I couldn't be sure, but I'd never had that happen before.

Eventually, they began reading off the names of seniors on the team, and one by one they'd run out onto the field. By the time it was my turn and I was up—I was already crying. I took off out of the tunnel, one last time, and reached Coach Meyer, who was also crying. So many moments that we would always remember. He would always be there in my life, but it was going to be different.

When the game started, I began hitting all my receivers. I played my best game of the year against FSU. We won with a final score of 37-10.

Behind a great offensive line, I threw three touchdown passes and ran for two more. I even fumbled late in the game at the end of a good play, but for once I didn't beat myself up too much about it. It still bothered me ... but it was a really awesome play.

It was good to beat them four times.

After the game, we went to the Hilton, where we'd planned a surprise celebration for my mom's birthday. Over 100 people attended the party, and it was an incredibly happy occasion on a day with both joy and sorrow. As good as it felt to beat FSU and end the regular season undefeated, it was hard to stop thinking about the fact that my college football career was ending soon. Of course, before that could happen, we had to face the biggest test so far that year.

The next week was the SEC Championship Game against Alabama.

They started the game off better than we did. We fell behind, but after every lead we came back. Unfortunately, we simply couldn't stop them. We trailed 12-10 in the second quarter and then 19-13 at the half. Looking back, I should have been more bothered than I was at halftime, but I was certain we would come back to win.

As the second half began, they played solid football. We just couldn't stop them enough. We ended up losing on a very long night, 32-13. They had the passion and focus and were the better team that night.

After the game, I was overwhelmed by emotion and could not hold back the tears. This wasn't how the season was supposed to go. Things weren't supposed to end here like this.

There was no bouncing back. We wouldn't be playing in the national championship.

The Alabama game is one that will always be with me. It'll always hurt like all the Saint Augustine losses while at Nease. To lose an SEC Championship Game, and an undefeated season, and a national championship, all at once . . . well that was tough.

Winning and doing well isn't always what God has in mind for us. People expect you to be a good winner, but they know how agonizing it is to lose. When you are able to shine during those times of great disappointment, it can have quite an impact. I try to keep that in mind.

I know that somewhere people may be watching you or me. How they see us handle the tough times that come into our lives could make a difference in how they handle something they face in their lives.

The next week, I went to Orlando for the Home Depot College Football Awards ceremony again, but I didn't expect to win since other guys had played better that year.

Sitting in a restaurant the night before the awards ceremony, I noticed a girl standing outside and pointing in my direction. Robby brought her and her family into the restaurant. I learned that her name was Kelly Faughnan and she had been diagnosed with a brain tumor the year before. After surgery, she had asked her parents if they could come to Disney for a vacation—and to hopefully meet me at the Home Depot Awards. I had an idea: Since I didn't have a date for the awards ceremony, I asked her if she'd attend the event with me.

We had a great night, talking and enjoying each other's company. At the end of the evening, I turned to my mom and said that, sure enough, I didn't win anything.

She paused, and I could tell that I was going to get some of Mom's wisdom.

"You had the best night of all."

Right again, Mom. Right again.

Going to the Heisman that weekend was fun, too. I had already won the Campbell Award, which is awarded for doing well in the classroom as well as on the field. It is often called the Academic Heisman. But we knew I wouldn't be winning the actual Heisman that year. I'm the only player who has ever been nominated for three of them, but I'm still not entirely sure why they even invited me. But I wasn't going to turn down another one of those fun New York family vacations.

After the fun, it was time to get back to work. We faced Cincinnati in the Sugar Bowl. They'd been highly ranked all year, but to be honest, I just didn't have the excitement and energy to play them. The same would have been true no matter who we faced. Our goal had been to play for the national championship. Anything less than that was a disappointment.

Still, we had a pretty decent few weeks of practice. It was important to me that we finish strong. Sometimes in life things don't work out as you'd hoped. How you respond is important. Do you hang your head and walk away, or do you find the next challenge and go for it?

I wanted us to go for it, to finish strong.

We did. We won, 51-24, and I passed for the most yards in my college career, 482. I ended up with 533 yards of rushing and passing combined, the most in the history of any BCS game. In addition, we became the first school to win thirteen games in back-to-back seasons.

Some think we showed that we were, in fact, the best team ever.

I was finished at the University of Florida. Like so many of the guys I was honored to play with and the coaches who coached us, I did the best I could, trying to always finish strong.

18

THE DRAFT AND DENVER

*Three things will last forever—faith, hope, and love—
and the greatest of these is love.*
—1 Corinthians 13:13 (NLT)

I HAD GRADUATED WITH HONORS from the University of Florida with a bachelor's degree in Family, Youth, and Community Sciences. I don't think I could've gotten more out of the college experience than I did.

By then, I had selected an agent for the next phase in my life, which I hoped would be a professional career in football—the NFL. After interviewing several agents, my family decided that Jimmy Sexton from Memphis, Tennessee, was the best fit for us.

I went to the Senior Bowl in Mobile, Alabama, to work out for the representatives from NFL teams who would be watching players and making decisions about who they wanted on their team.

At one point, I was in my hotel room signing autographs. My brothers were there with me, joking around. Suddenly, an ESPN commentator came on the television screen and said, "Tim Tebow is probably the fifth or sixth best quarterback in the 2010 draft." The room was instantly still and quiet, but I kept signing autographs. "You know how many guys he'll be choosing at the draft?" Robby asked, taking my side and hoping to make me feel better. "Zero."

I didn't care. Really. I'd heard that before. I was already working as hard as I could. I kept signing, and then we went to the weight room for a workout.

Somewhere he is out there . . .

As Jimmy kept reminding me, we didn't need to convince all thirty-two teams to pick me, only one. I was looking forward to improving in order to make it to the next level. Those improvements started immediately—I began working out in Nashville at a facility called D1 Sports Training.

I ran, I threw, I lifted, and I did a variety of drills to improve my body. I also looked for ways to improve the mental part of my game. Anything I could do to make myself better, I did. I threw thousands of passes of all distances, arcs, spin speeds, touches, and routes.

By late February, it was time for the NFL Combine. This was a gathering in Indianapolis, Indiana, of the top college football players. The NFL teams give players physical examinations; test their strength, speed, and agility; work them out in football drills; and interview them. I was pleased with my performance—especially on the three-cone drill, which is a test of quickness and agility. I had the fastest time of all the quarterbacks at the combine and third- or fourth-fastest overall.

And then after the combine, I went back to my regular workouts—more lifting, more running, more throwing.

On March 17, a ton of NFL folks attended Pro Day at the University of Florida. The scouts and coaches were also curious to see me and how I threw since I had chosen not to work on any passing drills at the combine. Instead I had wanted to continue working on my throwing motion.

Pro Day went well, I thought. At the end of the day, though, whether or not a quarterback is successful is based on how many wins and losses he has. I just needed a coach who believed in me and my abilities and who I am inside.

I didn't have to get *every* team to want to take me ...
just that *one*.

The NFL invited me to attend the draft in New York. I decided to stay in Jacksonville because I couldn't predict the round in which I would be selected. Plus, I wanted to be home with family and friends who had watched and been a part of this long journey with me.

Watching the draft at our friend Bryan Craun's house had become a yearly event for my brothers and me, so we kept the tradition going. This time, he hosted a big party that included guests from ESPN and the NFL Network. Another difference? It was the first time that we were listening for my name.

Jimmy predicted that Denver would take me somewhere toward the end of the first round. However, Denver used their first-round pick on a wide receiver near the end of the first round, so it didn't look like that would be the case.

In the meantime, the draft had been going on for hours—pick after pick, name after name. The excitement was still there, but people were nervous and tired. Would I be taken that night, or would I have to wait for the second round the next day—or later?

The phone rang. I looked down and saw a 303 area code. Denver.

I turned to Jimmy. "It's from 303. Should I answer it?" I knew who it was, but I didn't let my expression give it away.

Jimmy almost fell out of the chair, scrambling to his feet. "It's Denver! Answer it! Answer it! It's them!"

We still laugh about that.

It was Josh McDaniels, the head coach of the Denver Broncos. He told me that they were trading picks to move back into the first round and were selecting me. I was a Denver Bronco.

I rented a house with my brothers in Denver and began spending as much time as I could there, participating in every team activity. Robby helps handle activities in my life that aren't related to football, and Peter's in graduate school there.

Although I had hoped to start as quarterback from the beginning, the coaches made it clear that they didn't want to rush it. They wanted me to get used to the NFL first.

I started the Tim Tebow Foundation to carry on the work that we began with First and 15—to bring faith, hope, and love to those who are in need of a brighter day.

I kept working hard, learning as much as I could the best that I could. It's a challenge, being a backup in the NFL. You get very few repetitions in practice during the week. In other words, there aren't a lot of chances to repeat a play over and over again so you get better at it. Still, you need to be sharp and ready in case you play. As for me, I didn't play much at all for most of the year.

In our opening game, a loss to the Jaguars in Jacksonville, I rushed twice for two yards and didn't play again for five weeks. Then, against the New York Jets, I rushed six times for twenty-three yards, including my first NFL touchdown. The following week, I ran for another touchdown against the 49ers in a game that we played at Wembley Stadium in London. Two weeks later, I threw my first NFL touchdown pass and ran for another against the Chiefs.

While I was pleased to be contributing, it was hard to watch from the sidelines while Kyle Orton was quarterbacking. I hoped to have my role expand, of course. I knew I could do well if they'd just give me the chance.

As the season progressed, we struggled to win games. After thirteen weeks of the season, we were 3-9, and Josh McDaniels was fired. His firing was distressing. Josh believed in me enough to draft me. On the other hand, he didn't play me much. Since we weren't having a successful season, I didn't understand why. Playing me would not have been a big risk. But I also realized that the NFL is different, and Josh, the coaches, and management wanted to give me every opportunity to learn and grow in order to be successful. And so I continued to learn, work hard, and support Kyle and the team and, occasionally when I got in the game, do whatever I could do to help make us successful.

Josh's firing brought attention to me, too. People began guessing right away that I might not remain in Denver for long, because Coach McDaniels, my biggest supporter, was gone.

I didn't have time to focus on that. Instead, I dealt with the uncertainty the way that I've always tried to: I don't know what the future holds, but I know Who holds my future. That's what gives me hope and peace and is what I lean on. I know that no matter what happens, there's a plan for it, and even though I don't always understand it all and why things happen the way they do, I know that one day it will all make sense as a part of God's plan. Even if it doesn't turn out the way that I hope, it will be disappointing but I'll be all right, because God never stops loving me, or you. And God will use every one of those things—some of which may seem good and some bad to us at the time—in His overall plan for your life and mine.

Finally, in week fifteen, I started my first NFL game in Oakland against the Raiders.

It was a challenge for all of us, because Kyle and I have very different styles, and the offense had been chosen with his skills in mind.

It was rainy and muddy. Fun football conditions.

In the first quarter, I made a mistake. The other coaches called for a tailback draw, but instead I heard "quarterback draw." Maybe my subconscious knew that I wanted to run the ball.

I held on to the ball and ran for a forty-yard touchdown. On the play, I stiff-armed their safety just before reaching the end zone. Later that quarter, I threw a touchdown pass to Brandon Lloyd, who made a fantastic catch. With that play, I accomplished something that only two other players in NFL history had ever done: Throw a touchdown pass of thirty or more yards and run for a touchdown of forty or more yards in the same game.

Unfortunately, we lost the game, dropping us to 3-11. I'd never been on a team with a losing record. Ever. It was tough and not anything that I want to experience again.

The next week, we were facing the Houston Texans at home. The coaches had a week to prepare a game plan specifically for me, and we started off great. I was so excited to hear the Denver crowd react as we came onto the field. The cheers were so loud that I had to signal the crowd to quiet down so we could hear our snap count. That never happens at a home game.

We drove right down the field, and I completed my first two passing attempts. Then I threw a pass that was intercepted.

We didn't do anything else that is worth mentioning during the first half and went into the locker room at halftime trailing, 17-0. Early in the second half, I threw a fifty-yard pass to Jabar Gaffney, which led to our first touchdown. We each got a field goal, and then they added another. We ended the third quarter down 23-10.

Early in the fourth quarter, I threw a touchdown pass to Correll Buckhalter, and we trailed only 23-17. We got the ball back and began driving.

We reached their six yard line. Second down and goal. The coaches called for a fake quarterback draw to the right—I would pretend to run with the ball instead of passing it. Our receiver, Eddie Royal, was supposed to fake like he was blocking and then move to the goal-post for the pass.

I sent the running back into motion. He was supposed to go into motion to the left so we'd have three receivers to the right and two to the left. He went right instead. That resulted in four receivers to the right, with only one to the left. With the play clock running down, we had to snap it then figure out what to do. I took the snap and faked the quarterback draw, then began backing up. I hoped that a defender would come after me and open up a receiver for me to throw to. No one did. I was able to beat their left end to the outside. Because the defensive back covering Brandon Lloyd on that side of the field didn't turn around, I was able to slip into the end zone.

The fans were going crazy in the stands, and we were, too. We kicked the extra point and led 24-23. Minutes later, Syd'Quan Thompson intercepted a pass thrown by Matt Schaub, and we had our fourth win of the season. In the process, I threw for over 300 yards. It was a good day.

It was even more special because my entire family was there, including my nieces and nephew. We had all planned on being together that week, because Christmas was the day before the game. I had to stay in the team hotel on Christmas, so we actually celebrated two days after the game, on Tuesday the 28th.

A very merry Christmas for our family.

Our season finale was at home against the San Diego Chargers. My confidence was high, and it seemed that the coaches' and players' confidence in me had grown as well. I was particularly excited to face the Chargers—Philip Rivers is widely recognized as one of the best quarterbacks in the NFL.

We didn't get off to a great start. A receiver dropped a long pass on our opening drive, and then I threw an interception on the next play. Even so, Brandon Lloyd scored a touchdown on my pass in the first quarter, and we took an early 7-0 lead. However, by the third quarter, we trailed 23-7, and then 33-14 midway through the fourth.

On the next kickoff, Cassius Vaughn scored for us on a ninety-seven-yard return. Then with twenty-six seconds left, I scored on a run, bringing it to 33-28.

The crowd was frantic, hoping for another

miraculous finish. So were we. We ended up with two chances to win it. I threw two Hail Mary passes into the end zone, but both were knocked down by the Chargers. We lost, but had fought to the very end.

We were a 4-12 team. We had lost. And still the fans cheered as we left the field for the final time for the season. I think they appreciated the effort that the team showed in the loss.

The months since the end of the football season have been as busy and exciting as ever. Whenever I am not preparing for the upcoming football season, I am typically busy working on my foundation. Although the Tim Tebow Foundation is just getting under way, through the support of many generous people, we are already fulfilling dreams of children with life-threatening illnesses, partnering with deserving children's organizations throughout the United States and supporting over 600 orphans worldwide. There is no question that God has blessed me with a heart for children, and I fully intend to spend my free time working to bring faith, hope, and love to those in need.

As I've said before, I don't know what my future holds, but I do know that God holds my future. With that in mind, I seek to continue to live in a way that always brings glory to Him.

I hope my future includes football, at least for now. Football has always been my passion, and in one way or another, it will always be my passion. I simply pray that I will continue to have the privilege to reach out to and connect with others—and to inspire them through my faith in God.

So, that's my story—through my eyes. But as you can possibly tell, I believe we are called to view the world, and especially our relationships with those around us, through HIS eyes.

ACKNOWLEDGMENTS

God saved you by His grace when you believed. And you can't take credit for this; it is a gift from God. Salvation is not a reward for the good things we have done, so none of us can boast about it. —Ephesians 2:8-9 (NLT)

FIRST AND FOREMOST, I want to thank my Lord and Savior, Jesus Christ, for once again blessing me with a platform to share my story, which hopefully will influence others positively.

To Dad, because of your courage, you have inspired me to never settle and always press on.

To Mom, words cannot express how much you mean to me; you are a true example of a godly woman.

To my sisters and brothers-in-law:

Christy and Joey—thank you for teaching me the importance of sacrificing for God's work. You lead by example.

Katie and Gannon—I always have a brighter day when I'm with y'all. You always put a smile on my face.

To my brothers:

Robby—thank you for always looking out for and protecting me, you are so much more than a big brother to me. I couldn't do it without you.

Peter—thank you for being real and always reminding me to keep God first in my life.

To Uncle Bill, thank you for always being there for me, providing me with godly wisdom, and being like my second dad.

To Angel Gonzalez, I truly cherish our friendship. Thank you for your great ideas throughout this process, including coming up with the title, and your dedication to see the book through to completion.

To Coach Meyer, for believing in me and giving me a chance. I will forever treasure you and your family—y'all mean the world to me. Thank you for taking me in as a son. We had a great run.

To Kevin Albers, my best friend. Thanks for the memories. I'll always have your back—love you, Brother.

To Bryan Craun, thank you for your kindness, friendship, and unwavering support over the years. Make sure to keep that neck warm! Love you, CD5.

To Nathan Whitaker, thank you for everything. What I enjoyed the most was the transition from initially just being my coauthor to becoming my friend. I am also very grateful for the assistance of Nathan's mother, Lynda Whitaker, who transcribed our many hours of conversations, and his father, Scott Whitaker, who worked alongside him to craft the manuscript and make my words a reality in print.

To Matt Johnson, Wendy Kirk, DJ Snell, and Greg Suess, thank you for your expertise in guiding us through the logistics of creating a book.

To Lisa Sharkey, Matt Harper, Mark Tauber, Julie Burton, Margaret Anastas, Annie Stone, and the rest of the team at HarperCollins, thank you for your patience and professionalism in making this a book of which I'm proud.

QUESTIONS AND ANSWERS

1. Did you always know that you wanted to play professional football?

   I've dreamed about playing in the NFL since I was six years old. I remember watching my two favorite teams back then, the Florida Gators and the Dallas Cowboys, and dreaming about one day leading them down the field on game winning drives.

2. Were your parents nervous about you playing football?

   My mom was a little nervous, but my dad wasn't nervous at all. Ultimately, they both trusted God with my life and allowed me to pursue my dream.

3. What is your favorite thing to do in the off-season?

   Without a doubt, it's being able to spend time with my family.

4. What does it feel like to run into a stadium with 100,000 screaming fans?

Awesome. Whether they are cheering for you or against you, the fans are the best part of playing sports.

5. What player hit you the hardest?

Over the years I've had many hard collisions, but one guy that I went against year after year that always hit hard was Eric Berry, who played at the University of Tennessee and now plays for the Kansas City Chiefs.

6. What player did you most admire growing up?

I actually had two favorites: Danny Wuerffel and Emmitt Smith. I admired Danny for his humility and how he always carried himself, and Emmitt because he was the greatest running back I had ever seen. It also had something to do with the fact that they were both great Gators!

7. What was your first jersey number?

#7 (See photo on page 3 of the color insert)

8. What is the best present you ever got for your birthday?

   I've received a lot of cool presents over the years, but last year I received a gift that was probably my favorite; my brother Robby gave me my dog, Bronco.

9. Was it your idea to wear Bible verses on your eye black? Are you disappointed that you can't do it anymore since there was such a great response to it?

   Yes, it was my idea, because I thought that the eye black was a great way to express my faith and share my favorite verses not only with my teammates and fans, but also to serve as a constant reminder for me of how blessed I am. I would not say that I am disappointed but rather challenged to find other, more creative ways to share my faith ... GB²

10. Where do you see yourself in ten years?

    I want to be working hard as a successful professional quarterback and have my foundation grow beyond my wildest dreams.